A SHORT INTRODUCTION TO INTERNATIONAL LAW

In our globalised world the sources and actors of international law are many and its growth prolific and disorderly. International law governs the actions of states on matters as long-standing as diplomatic immunity or as recent as the 'War on Terror', and it now impacts upon the lives of ordinary citizens in areas as diverse as banking and investment, public health and the protection of the environment. In this accessible introduction Emmanuelle Tourme Jouannet explains the latest developments in international law in the light of its history and culture, presenting it as an instrument both for dominance and for change that adjusts and balances the three pillars of the United Nations Charter: the prohibition of the use of force; economic, social and sustainable development; and human rights.

EMMANUELLE TOURME JOUANNET is Professor of International Law at the Sciences Po Paris School of Law. Among the most prominent French international law scholars of her generation, she is the author of many publications, including two books in English: *The Liberal-Welfarist Law of Nations: A History of International Law* (Cambridge, 2012) and *What is a Fair International Society? International Law between Development and Recognition* (2013). She is also one of the editors-in-chief of the *Journal of the History of International Law*.

A SHORT INTRODUCTION TO INTERNATIONAL LAW

EMMANUELLE TOURME JOUANNET

Translated from the French

Le Droit International (Presses Universitaires de France, 2013)

BY CHRISTOPHER SUTCLIFFE

CAMBRIDGE
UNIVERSITY PRESS

University Printing House, Cambridge CB2 8BS, United Kingdom

Cambridge University Press is part of the University of Cambridge.

It furthers the University's mission by disseminating knowledge in the pursuit of education, learning and research at the highest international levels of excellence.

www.cambridge.org
Information on this title: www.cambridge.org/9781107451360

© 2013 Presses Universitaires de France, *Le droit international*

This publication is in copyright. Subject to statutory exception and to the provisions of relevant collective licensing agreements, no reproduction of any part may take place without the written permission of Cambridge University Press.

First published in French by Presses Universitaires de France 2013
First published by Cambridge University Press 2014

Printed in the United Kingdom by Clays, St Ives plc

A catalogue record for this publication is available from the British Library

Library of Congress Cataloging in Publication data
Jouannet, Emmanuelle
[Droit international. French]
A short introduction to international law / Emmanuelle Tourme Jouannet; translated from the French Le Droit International (Presses Universitaires de France, 2013) by Christopher Sutcliff.
    pages cm
Includes index.
ISBN 978-1-107-08640-1 (hardback) – ISBN 978-1-107-45136-0 (paperback)
1. International law.   I. Title.
KZ3410.J6814   2014
341 – dc23   2014033375

ISBN 978-1-107-08640-1 Hardback
ISBN 978-1-107-45136-0 Paperback

To my children

CONTENTS

vii

INTRODUCTION

International law is an international policy instrument. It is a set of rules, discourses and techniques that its subjects and actors use to regulate their relations and accomplish certain social ends. International law has its own culture and history. It has evolved over several centuries to reach its current form, and is: a fundamental process for regulating and channelling international violence; an essential common language; an instrumental technique in the service of states and of all the actors of international society. It is a promise of peace. In all of this, its force of attraction is very real indeed. But ever since it emerged in the modern era, international law has also been a part of a profoundly unequal international society in which it nurtures as much violence as it appeases. Far from being a straightforward neutral legal technique, it is, and always has been, the projection upon the international stage of the values and interests of international society's main players, at the same time being used by groups resisting that dominant order. In this respect, it is intrinsically ambivalent. It is simultaneously an instrument of domination and an instrument of emancipation for the subjects and actors who use it. It is as much the sword of the mighty as it is the shield of the meek.

International law has changed considerably since 1945, and its many-faceted development contrasts starkly with the uniformity of classical law. We are witnessing a contemporary multiplication of the sources, norms, operators and users of international law, while the role of sovereign states, until now the foundation of this law, is becoming decidedly less absolute. It is now the law of an international society that emerged from the Second World War and has become a post-colonial and post-Cold War society. These three episodes account for some of the most essential shifts it has undergone. In particular, the classical representation of international law laying down the rules to govern a mosaic of juxtaposed sovereign states is no longer tenable and no longer fits contemporary international law. Sovereignty has weakened, and international institutions, individuals and private economic actors are ever more emancipated in our globalised world. International law is changing and its traditional dividing lines are being redrawn to accommodate new structures, areas of regulation and intervention, subjects, content and scope.

International law is therefore a body of law undergoing wholesale change as the limits of the classical dogmatic presentation of it become apparent everywhere. This change, though, raises many issues of its own that must also be weighed up. International law is currently expanding and evolving in response to unprecedented demand. But it is evolving beyond recognition and control. This paradox is confirmed if we try to discern its most distinctive features more clearly, and it has led me to multiply the angles of approach to this system of law rather than to close in on it from just one direction, a move that might restrict the perspective and skew our understanding. I propose to contemplate international law from three separate vantage points as a way of identifying and discussing its most essential dimensions: international law as history and culture (Chapter 1); international law as a legal order (Chapter 2); and international law as an instrument of social regulation and intervention (Chapter 3). These three dimensions will enable me to bring out some of the most important issues which international law has raised in different places and at different times, and to critically examine those features, both old and new, that confer on it its legal character.

1

International law as history and culture

International law is a human practice punctuated by a series of changes that have affected its forms and meanings in a process that has been neither linear nor one-directional. It has continually stirred up controversies about its existence and its nature, some of which have become long-standing, others outmoded. International law is comparatively recent law, in that it did not really emerge with the Treaties of Westphalia of 1648 (even if its historiography often cites that date) but later, in the eighteenth century when modern Europe was in its heyday. In this, it is a culture, a European (and more broadly Western) culture, in which law is given an eminent position in the realm of political thought. Ever since the eighteenth century, international law has sought to rule a diverse, plural international society in which resources are unequally shared among states, and populations and individuals are unequally endowed in terms of their wealth, freedom and well-being.

International law was first known as the law of nations before it came to be referred to more frequently as international law in the nineteenth and twentieth centuries. It came into being at the same time as the modern state was being consolidated in Europe, and its initial purpose was to govern the legal rights and duties of states which were considered to be the only subjects of international law. However, it was to be applied to just a small group of European and American states who regarded themselves as the only ones capable of benefiting from international law. It was therefore to exclude three-quarters of the planet for more than two centuries, thereby establishing discrimination among states in terms of their legal standing that is inseparable from its history. Three characteristic features of its historical evolution shall be surveyed here: it was a liberal pluralist system of law made up of a hard core of fundamental rights and duties of states (section I); it authorised states to resort to war individually as a means of settling disputes (section II); and it was reserved to those states that were considered civilised, so making European colonisation of the rest of the world lawful (section III).

I. A liberal pluralist system of law

The liberal pluralist purpose of classical international law hinged entirely upon the principle of the sovereign state as the sole subject and juristic entity of international law. That purpose was characterised by four distinguishing features that were common to almost all legal discourse and practice from the mid-eighteenth until the mid-twentieth centuries.

First, classical international law was erected on the foundation stone of state sovereignty and freedom. Johann Ludwig Klüber wrote in 1819, 'The state is a *free* and *independent* society since it is made up of individuals and families who, without this association, would live in natural freedom and who have themselves proposed the goal which is the subject of their union.'[1]

---

[1] J. L. Klüber, *Droit des gens moderne de l'Europe*, Stuttgart: J. G. Cotta, 1819, vol. 1, pp. 66–7. Emphasis added.

The sovereignty of the state as a subject of international law was characterised in the ordinary discourse of international law primarily as a form of freedom and not a form of power. Sovereignty reflected the independence of states and was therefore an anti-hegemonic principle in the international arena. Sovereignty was the legal construct that at the outset prohibited any claim in law by another state, the Pope, or the Holy Roman Emperor to dominate others, and international law was liberal in that it aimed to limit the power of states at the same time as it aimed to ensure their freedom.

Second, the will of the state became the primary source of classical international law accounting for state responsibility, state recognition, the importance of the institution of promising and above all the power to enter into treaties. In much the same way as a man, as the sovereign of his own person, can freely enter into contracts, the free and independent sovereign state had the power to bind itself by a meeting of minds. From the nineteenth century onwards, international treaties were considered to be an essential source of classical international law, every bit as important as the principles of natural law had been since the eighteenth century. It was the age of great doctrinal codification, and legal positivism was becoming dominant. Like Francis Lieber in 1863, Jean Gaspard Bluntschli in 1868 or Pasquale Fiore in 1890, authors compiled codes, setting down in writing the international law of their time. It was also the period in which treatises and textbooks proliferated, standardising people's perception of international law.

Third, classical liberal international law was characterised by the principle of neutrality, which was sometimes referred to as the principle of tolerance. International law was held to be neutral with regard to the political and religious choices made by states in their domestic orders. It authorised and guaranteed the pluralism of internal political regimes, which might be conservative or liberal, democratic or monarchic. It was also oblivious as to whether individual liberties were observed within each state, and to any state religion, which was a very significant issue at the time. The legal technique that gave substance to this liberal principle of neutrality was quite straightforward. It consisted in dissociating state sovereignty into internal and external sovereignty. This crucial distinction had previously existed but now it was used to trace a dividing line between international law as a strictly external law of relations among states and public law as the internal law of each state. It therefore reduced international law in the nineteenth century to a mere system of law operative among states and external sovereignties, and it left states completely free in terms of their internal sovereignty over their own territory with regard to their own citizens.

The strictly inter-state logic that thus came about was crucial because it was to erect sovereignty as an impenetrable screen for the state behind which none would have any right of scrutiny, supervision or intervention. This resulted in the constant reiteration of the principle of non-intervention in states' internal affairs and soon in the rejection by most international law scholars and politicians of the principle of monarchic legitimacy laid down by the 1815 Vienna Congress. Indeed, all Europe's liberal regimes were to construct themselves *against* the 1815 principle of legitimacy. It is common knowledge that in the wake of the victory over Napoleon, Europe's sovereigns met in Vienna to rebuild Europe on the double foundations of the principle of legitimacy and the political arrangements of the *Ancien Régime*. The absolutist rulers sought to snuff out any revolutionary movement by forming the celebrated Holy Alliance. Yet European history of the ensuing years marks the gradual destruction of this 1815 order by aspirations to liberalism and nationality. Shaken by the revolutionary waves of 1830 and 1848, the order of 1815 finally collapsed in the second half of the nineteenth century. From then on, no basic textbook of international law continued to defend the principle of legitimacy or the right of intervention that went along with it. In conformance with what has become standard practice, commentators presented the principle of monarchic legitimacy as obsolete in view of the internal transformation of European monarchies into liberal regimes. International law therefore no longer busied itself with states' municipal sovereignty and with what was significantly coming to be called their 'internal' or 'reserved domain'. Intervention in another state's 'internal affairs' was unanimously condemned as a violation of the law of nations. Humanitarian intervention alone survived and, as we know, was to have a bright future. But intervention was only undertaken with respect to non-Europeans and it justified, for example, expeditions by European powers against the Ottoman Empire in 1827, China in 1900 and Morocco in 1909, and France's expedition against Syria in 1860. Interference and intervention among European and civilised states were still formally condemned.

Fourth, classical international law was a liberal law because it was also a formal law of negative coexistence of free sovereign states. The crucial importance accorded to state freedom and sovereignty, to states' will, to the neutrality of law and to pluralism among states made the observance of the individual rights of states imperative over any other considerations or requirements. These were rights and freedoms of which the state could avail itself against any other state seeking to restrict its power of intervention or action, and which rested ultimately on the rule of respect for the equal freedom and sovereignty of others. One state's freedom ended where the freedom of others began. All of classical international law was to be articulated around the celebrated doctrine of the fundamental rights and duties of states. This doctrine, which fully codified practice, was to meet with unbelievable success throughout the nineteenth and twentieth centuries up until the Second World War. It gave precedence to states' rights over their duties towards others, and it drew a distinction between their absolute rights and their secondary and relative rights. Absolute rights prevailed under any circumstances by the simple fact that a political entity was constituted into a state. These rights were permanent and untouchable, whereas relative rights were contingent and dependent on circumstances and treaties made among states. Absolute rights, the crux of the theory, were also called fundamental rights of states. Their definition varied between authors and with state discourse but usually included the famous rights of self-preservation of the state: respect for sovereignty, territorial integrity, trade and equality. In return, by a simple effect of symmetry, states had the absolute duty to respect these rights in their dealings with other states.

Underpinning this paradigmatic doctrine of fundamental rights was the concept of the legal personality of the state. It was once again taken up by all the classical commentators and considered central, even to the extent that some international law scholars theorised a right to 'respect of states' personality'.[2] The concept commanded the condition of legal independence of the state and the necessary observance of its consubstantial rights by other states. The personality of the state meant more specifically that it was likened to an individual being (despite its corporative character) who remained the exclusive subject of classical international law. The Italian international law scholar P. Fiore expounded this very clearly by claiming that the state had both 'international individuality and personality'.[3]

All told, such a liberal pluralist system of law concerning states as sovereign moral entities which were independent and equal, perfectly encapsulated a system of individual freedoms. It was conceived of as a law of formal *limits* designed to ring-fence and ensure the interplay of freedoms and sovereignties. The exercise of the rights and duties pertaining to the sovereignty of each state was not to interfere with other states' enjoyment of the reciprocal sovereign rights and duties. In this, international law was initially instituted to counter any

---

[2] A.-W. Heffter, *Le droit international public de l'Europe*, Berlin: Schroeder and Paris: Cotillon, 1866, p. 4.

[3] P. Fiore, *Nouveau droit international public suivant les besoins de la civilisation moderne*, translated and annotated by C. Antoine, 2nd edn, Paris: A. Durand et Pedone-Lauriel, 1885, p. 323.

hegemonic practice directed at them. It aimed for relations among states to be organised not for the benefit of any single sovereign (Pope, Holy Roman Empire, most powerful state, etc.) but in the interests of all and respecting the plurality of choices of each. International law thereby primarily fulfilled the expectations of the low- and medium-ranking European states of the time (which were the majority) because state sovereignty and the rights and duties attached thereto were in this respect liberating and emancipating.

Yet as Montesquieu wrote in the eighteenth century, freedom is also bound up with security and the feeling of safety.[4] The same was true of the sovereignty and freedom of European states. The problem was that the society which sovereign states formed together was fragile because, short of there being a *Civitas Maxima* or court of law for nations, that society was more like an anarchic state of nature in which the rights of each sovereign state were often violated by the continuation of power politics and war among states. The liberal purpose of international law was therefore to become twofold from the start, as in any liberal system. The law of nations was also to have as its purpose the preservation of the security of all states so as to guarantee the freedom and sovereignty of each state. This purpose was particularly difficult to achieve, though, because until 1945 classical international law authorised the use of war as a possible means of dispute settlement. Therein lay the paradox of an international (Euro-American) society that sought to ensure the security of sovereign states through the law but which was to maintain an essential role for war.

---

[4] Montesquieu, *De l'esprit des lois*, Paris: Flammarion, 2008, XI, 3, p. 54.

II. The lawfulness of the individual use of force as a means of dispute settlement

The liberal dimension of the law of nations was intrinsically wound up with the feeling of insecurity and violence within Europe which the law of nations did as much to curb as it did to legitimise. The celebrated Thirty Years War, which ravaged Europe from 1618 to 1648, bled it dry. This conflict lived on in the memories of eighteenth-century Europeans as a war of unprecedented ferocity. It was precisely this warlike atmosphere that led the Dutch jurisconsult Hugo Grotius to write his renowned *De Iure Belli ac Pacis* which is held to be the first great treatise on the law of nations but which in fact focused fully on war and the legal means to limit it.

> I, for the reasons which I have stated, holding it to be most certain that there is among nations a common law of Rights which is of force with regard to war, and in war, saw many and grave causes why I should write a work on that subject. For I saw prevailing throughout the Christian world a license in making war, of which even barbarous nations would have been ashamed; recourse was had to arms for slight reasons, or for no reason; and when arms were once taken up, all reverence for divine and human law was thrown away; just as if men were thenceforth authorized to commit all crimes without restraint.[5]

Classical international law was to remain entwined with the law of war which was to be both codified and limited, and formed

---

[5] W. Whewell, *Grotius on the rights of war and peace. An abridged translation*, Cambridge: Parker 1853. Prolegomena, art. 28.

one of the most important branches of law. Up until the inter-war years (1918–39), the individual security of each state was sought rather than international peace, and that authorised each state to use force to defend itself and its rights. This took on a double form. The principle of neutrality was a first form: the tolerance of classical international law with regard to the nature of internal political regimes and religious beliefs was already a liberal process for neutralising violence and stabilising society, because it prohibited any intervention on those grounds. It was logically associated with the principles of non-intervention and non-interference in a state's domestic affairs.

The second form was the demarcation of the right to wage war. This was more ambivalent, though, because it was also a potential source of violence. It should be emphasised that from the eighteenth century onwards, when international law truly emerged, the law of war was radically transformed. It was the time when the old idea of just war was definitively abandoned by jurisconsults and European powers. The recourse to war remained lawful but only for sovereign states, and it was modified in three ways. First, the idea was definitively abandoned that there had necessarily to be a just cause for waging war for it to be lawful under the law of nations. So long as two states waged war in the forms of the modern law of nations, it was considered that each had a just cause, since there was no court in the world to settle the matter. The war was deemed to be just on both sides. For that matter, the expression 'just war' was soon to be replaced by 'formal war' or 'regulated war', fought solely between states and lawful by that fact alone. Second, the legal regime of just war that had had devastating consequences for European security no longer applied. When a war was just, third parties were duty bound to intervene in favour of whoever had just cause, thus extending conflicts without end. From the mid-eighteenth century onwards, third parties had to remain neutral, and the early developments on the law of neutrality ensued. Third, just war had asymmetric effects. It accorded *temperamenta* – humane treatment of *ius in bello* – exclusively to those whose state claimed to have just cause, while almost any kind of treatment was meted out to those whose cause was unjust. This side did not have the benefit of any international humanitarian law. Now, with the new law of war, the effects of *ius in bello* were to be enjoyed on both sides.

The old doctrine of just war was therefore left aside with the emergence of first modern then classical international law. Even so, the right to wage war was not ruled out, and fitted in with the liberal framework of the theory of the state's fundamental rights as a means of self-defence and of dispute settlement. It was a fundamental and subjective right of the sovereign state and an essential attribute of its sovereignty. Because respect for their sovereign freedom was enshrined by classical international law, states had the legal option of deciding individually and therefore subjectively whether to resort to war (*ius ad bellum*) in order to recover their right or at least to obtain reparation for wrongs caused by some third party. Admittedly, it should be emphasised that there was nothing absolute about this *ius ad bellum* as it remained strictly governed by classical international law, which remained highly codified in this area until the inter-war period when it was placed under the aegis of the League of Nations. True, it must also be emphasised that the law in war (*ius in bello*) was to be made substantially more humane from the eighteenth century onwards, notably with the major conventions on international humanitarian law of The Hague in the late nineteenth and early twentieth centuries. They introduced legal limits as to what was lawful behaviour during wartime, and prohibited superfluous evils and inhumane conduct. But for all that, under classical international law, the decision to go to war remained lawful in the absence of a centralised system for the use of international force that might substitute for a state's individual right to wage war. It was unfortunately not until the trauma of the Second World War that this essential feature of the classical model finally came to an end.

Through its unprecedented scale, the First World War had already begun to bring about change to the issue of security, and classical international law was keenly criticised on this point. Aspiration to world peace became the fundamental provision of internationalist discourse and was unanimously celebrated by international law scholars with the ending of the war. It was a time when courses on the 'General Rules of the Law of Peace', from which the law of war was quite simply excluded, flourished at the new Academy of International Law in The Hague. Obviously nineteenth-century textbooks dealt with peace but certainly not in the same way, since it was above all the individual security of each state that was sought and achieved by whatever means necessary. Yet in the 1920s and 30s, the issue of peace was addressed on a worldwide and collective scale, and an avalanche of studies covered the law of peace, as if the repetition or incantation of doctrine might throw up a rampart against war. In fact, criticism of the time was often exaggerated and too quick to dismiss classical international law. In an overhasty amalgam, commentators inferred that states were legally entitled to spark any war at any time. However, nothing could have been further from the truth. Under classical international law, the right to resort to war was no more the right to do whatever one liked than sovereignty itself was absolute. On the eve of the First World War there were strict rules governing the use of armed force. The problem at the time was not the absence of legal limits on the right to resort to war, for there were such limits, but rather the absence of *control* over the states' exercise of their option to make a subjective interpretation of the situation and so of the decision to resort to war. This absence led to the introduction in 1919 of an international organisation, the League of Nations, and the principle of control by the Council of the League of Nations (arts. 12 to 16), which could even lead to joint action to prevent or overcome armed aggression. The idea of 'collective security' thus became one of the central principles of the new system which corrected the excessively liberal trajectory of classical law. The security of nations could no longer be ensured in a subjective or individualistic framework but had to be upheld within an institutional, joint and several, collective framework that could restrict states' capacity to make their own judgment on whether to resort to war.

However, the new institutionalised system was limited because war remained a lawful means not only of defending oneself but also of righting a wrong. Only the 1928 Briand–Kellog Pact of Paris fully banned its use, but the pact was to be ineffective. As a result, despite notable advances the legal system of security put in place by the Euro-Americans in the eighteenth and nineteenth centuries did not disappear with the League of Nations. Classical international law continued to hold sway and to maintain security by protecting and ensuring the individual rights of states and their existence as sovereign states, and by providing for war as the ultimate means of sanction or reparation.

Concern for security and the right to wage war were therefore added to the sovereign will and freedom of the state, and enshrined alongside individual rights and the neutrality of law. These components were distinguishing features which, when interconnected, gave classical international law its authority to govern the conduct of sovereign states and manage their conflicts on an equal footing. However, this international law was at the same time deeply discriminatory because it applied to just a small group of states which considered themselves to be civilised to the exclusion of all others. This was the darkest side of international law in that it was thus a legal instrument in the service of exploitation, imperialism and colonisation. It therefore saw a reversal of the situation in that while it was a liberal pluralist law in Europe, it was to become a hegemonic and anti-liberal law elsewhere in the world.

III. The law of civilised nations

The classical international law presented above was a system of law produced by liberal Euro-American law of the eighteenth and nineteenth centuries. At the time, all the world's regions had different ways of governing foreign relations among peoples, but it was the Euro-American legal system that was to impose itself on the rest of the planet through successive colonisations during the nineteenth and twentieth centuries. In the course of two centuries, Europe extended its power to the entire planet, with irreversible and tragic consequences for the world. This undertaking of colonial domination had multiple causes, both inside and outside Europe, including the industrial, technological and commercial take-off of Europe, the will to power and greatness of nation states, and their determination to control geographical space by way of capitalism, nationalism and multiple intra-European rivalries. By the late nineteenth century, Europe dominated almost the entire world both through colonial settlement, when vast territories in Australia and North and South America came under the control of populations of European origin, and through the colonial exploitation of Africa and much of Asia where a system of colonial administration or protectorates was imposed without a mass influx of colonists. International law, which was European by culture, was to legitimise the situation by introducing a distinction between civilised states, which were subjects of international law, and uncivilised or semi-civilised peoples, who were not subjects of international law and had to endure the domination of civilised states in order to gain access to the benefits of civilisation. It was the time when some international law scholars thought of themselves as the organ of the civilised legal conscience of the world.

Contrary to the liberal pluralist model governing relations among Euro-American states and states admitted to the circle of civilised nations on an equal footing, the legal relations which Europe was to forge with the rest of the world were based on dependence and inequality. International law scholar Antoine Pillet bluntly asserted in 1894 that 'there is no equality of rights between civilised states and uncivilised or less civilised states . . . *Between the condition of the ones and the condition of the others, there is a flagrant inequality and this inequality is, in this matter, the true basis of their relations.*[6] The legal reversal that ensued was complete, because the system of law that Europe brought with it instigated, reinforced and justified the superiority of law and power for the benefit of Europeans which ran directly counter to the liberal principles of neutrality, equality and freedom. Freedom of trade, which had been enshrined as a fundamental right of the state, became the spearhead of economic exploitation of non-Europeans. The technique of the treaty as the prime instrument for expressing the will of equal and sovereign states gave rise to the profoundly discriminatory practice of unequal treaties in which one of the two parties voluntarily accepted unequal obligations to its own detriment. The unfettered sovereignty of one side imposed a protected sovereignty on the other, as illustrated by the celebrated French protectorate treaties in Tunisia and Morocco, whereas international society as a whole formed a hierarchy between civilised, semi-civilised and uncivilised nations and not a multicentric society based on equality. In other words, the rules were no longer based on formal equality among states but, on the contrary, took account of ethnic and cultural differences and actual inequality of material, economic and social situations of certain peoples to justify the intervention of certain states with regard to some particular peoples or some

---

[6] A. Pillet, 'Le droit international public. Ses éléments constitutifs, son domaine, son objet', *Revue Générale de Droit International Public* (1894) 24–5. Emphasis added.

inferior types of state. These were interventionist rules that included the existence of special rights, the system of capitulations, international and colonial protectorates, appropriation of land and the exercise of external sovereignty, or even internal sovereignty in which uncivilised peoples were administered directly by a colonising state. In this last instance, the rules entitled civilised states to legally represent uncivilised peoples, to compel them to adopt a certain form of justice, administration, police, health, education, culture and trade. Dealing only with the most general aspects of these questions, these rules of international law were supplemented by the colonial legislation of European states and, accordingly, they relied on a power structure designed for the work of colonising and civilising the world.

This classical international law, in as much as it was pure Euro-American history and culture, began to be seriously challenged in the inter-war years. But it was only after 1945 and the introduction of the United Nations Charter that it underwent any real change. Contemporary international law exhibits several features that reflect, in a complex way, both its past legacy and its current rooting in the post-Second World War, post-colonial and post-Cold War world. This is the context for new requirements that are often included in contemporary international law, and helps to explain the growing importance of international law in national and international societies. Even so, we must better understand what these requirements and changes truly represent for international law, because however obvious they may seem to some, they have nonetheless been contested by others. This means we need to identify the essence of contemporary international law and be more specific about its current content by studying in succession and with a critical eye its general character as a legal system, and its purposes and material areas of application as an instrument of regulation and social intervention.

2

International law as a legal order

As a European cultural project, it is no surprise that international law exhibits a Western legal character. In particular, since it first emerged in the eighteenth century, it has been doctrinally conceived of in a systematised form typical of Western thought. It reflects the determination to impose a rationalised *order* among states upon what might appear to be the social *disorder* of international society and national societies. Envisioning international law as forming a legal order requires the consideration of it as an autonomous and coordinated set of subjects, institutions, practices and rules. This perception takes on even more importance within the discipline when the very concept of legal order becomes a common concept of the theory of law, as it did in the early twentieth century. Scholars realised how convenient it was for the understanding of international law to envisage it in the round and not just its various parts, because by doing so a whole series of questions about its definition, existence and validity (and those of its component parts) found a priori more helpful answers.

It is proposed to adhere to this vision of international law as a legal order because it is still of sufficient interest to present international law synthetically – from a legal and sociological standpoint and not one of formal logic – while at the same time showing its fragility and vulnerability to numerous challenges. Three questions will be specifically addressed. The first is a problem of the definition of international law and how it stands apart from other bodies of law and legal orders (section II). The second question is to identify some of its main components, that is, its subjects and its rules, because their increasing diversity is both a cause and an effect of the changes it is undergoing (section III). The third question is to enquire into its possible unity and coherence as a legal order, whereas it seems to be heading inexorably towards ever greater normative and institutional disorder (section IV). But before that, we shall recall a particularly keen debate that runs through all international disciplines: whether the changes since 1945 signal the end or the decline of the older classical legal order and the emergence of a new markedly different order (section I).

I. The debate about the end of the classical inter-state order

Contemporary international law is the law in force today which began in the aftermath of the Second World War, most notably with the adoption of the United Nations Charter as the outcome of the San Francisco Conference on 26 June 1945. International law has changed considerably since that time. Several new and particularly salient phenomena have appeared since 1945 that have incontrovertibly affected it – the spread and collapse of communist regimes, the development of international organisations, especially the United Nations family, the abolition of the right to wage war, decolonisation and the enshrinement of the rights of peoples to self-determination, the international recognition of human rights, the end of the Cold War and the advent of the latest neoliberal episode of globalisation.

All of these have intensified the breakdown of the classical categories on which international law was erected – the distinction between public and private, municipal and international, the hierarchical domestic order and the multicentric international order, the state as subject and the individual or people as object, the principle of equivalence between rules, and the distinction between national needs and international interests.

Accordingly, contemporary international law scholars have had to become accustomed to covering less familiar ground and rethinking their subject matter. Commentators have argued about whether this international law stands apart from the classical inter-state legal order briefly described (also known as the Westphalian model from the name of the Treaties of Westphalia of 1648) and whether it corresponds therefore to the emergence of a new legal order. For example, for Antonio Cassese or Georges Abi-Saab, a difference should now be drawn between the classical (Westphalian) model based on the liberal pluralism of sovereign states and the legal and political model that arose from the 1945 Charter and that supposedly corresponds to new objectives of the international community, with the emergence of human rights and the rights of peoples on the international level.[1] It is arguably, then, from 1945 onward that a new international order was truly introduced. The arguments of James N. Rosenau first published in 1990 were the starting point for another type of analysis, which

---

[1] A. Cassese, *Le droit international dans un monde divisé*, Paris: Berger-Levrault, 1986, pp. 185 ff and G. Abi-Saab, 'Cours général de droit international public', (1987) VII, vol. 207 *Recueil des Cours de l'Académie de Droit International*, pp. 319 ff.

dated the abandonment of the classical inter-state system to the advent of the latest episode of globalisation.[2] Rosenau takes the view that it was not in 1945 but instead with the globalisation after the Cold War that the inter-state model disappeared. For him, the old international system came apart from the 1990s onwards because of the far-reaching 'turbulence' of the post-Cold War world, which gave rise to a host of players and networks acting outside the framework of sovereignty. For other commentators, these different arguments about the abandonment of the classical inter-state model are all equally false and illusory, since in international law 'change is no novelty',[3] and the changes since 1945 or since 1989 could not have been a major challenge to the existing international system which is still thought of as structurally organised around coexistence and cooperation among sovereign states.

In point of fact, there is no simple answer to this question of the change in the legal order relative to the classical inter-state model, since it all depends on how one looks at the history of international law and at international law itself. This ultimately refers back to the cultural representations of each commentator but also to the academic and political schools to which observers belong. Familiar divides are found between realists and liberals, Continentals and Anglo-Saxons,

---

[2] J. N. Rosenau, *Turbulence in world politics. A theory of change and continuity*, Princeton University Press, 1990.

[3] G. Fitzmaurice, 'The future of international law and of the international legal system in the circumstances of today', in *Institut de droit international – Livre du centenaire*, Basel: Karger, 1973, p. 207 and P. Weil, *Ecrits de droit international*, Paris: Presses Universitaires de France, 2000, pp. 8 ff.

conservatives and progressives, and the global North and South. My own interpretation is that contemporary international law is incontrovertibly the outcome of a great deal of 'turbulence' in the post-1945, post-colonial and post-Cold War world, as these were three international contexts that profoundly altered the simple perception of the classical inter-state order that had prevailed until then. But the scope of those transformations must not be overstated since we are witnessing, for the time being at any rate, a mere *reconfiguration* of international law, that is, a transformed (reconfigured) combination of classical and new legal principles and practices. There is neither a radical break nor any repetition of a structure but rather an overlapping of old and new legal models, with the result that the old subjects and old practices still survive, including through the new subjects and new legal principles. We are not seeing one system of law definitively replacing another, but rather slippage, a shift towards a new model of international law that is becoming increasingly dominant while overlapping with the old model. Much of the tension, contradiction and uncertainty surrounding contemporary international law arise from this inevitable entwinement of new and old, between the classical inter-state order and the new legal order.

II. Definitions and distinctions

While contemporary international law is not radically new, even so it is undergoing a crisis of identity because of major changes that have occurred since 1945. This crisis is readily perceptible when one seeks to isolate the criteria by which it can be defined as a system of law – thereby distinguishing it from other systems of law – and which sometimes cause confusion over whether it is a legal order.

Definition of international law

The concept of international law has become increasingly difficult to pin down. International law was long defined as the system of law governing relations between states, or as the law of international society. But these classical definitions have grown obsolete since they only partially reflect what contemporary international law is, so much have its object, scope and content changed. To say that international law is an inter-state law, a law governing relations between states only, is false because international law also governs the conduct of subjects of law other than states, such as international organisations and individuals. To characterise international law as the law of international society is also too narrow a definition if it means that it governs only relations between subjects/actors of international relations. International law remains the system of law of international society; but it is also largely the law of internal societies, and governs domestic situations that have no international or foreign elements.

The following definition may be suggested in place of the traditional definitions, and is now commonly proposed to students. International law is composed of the set of legal rules, practices and discourses arising from the subjects of international law. It is law produced by the input of several international subjects. In other words, it is defined principally by its international *origin* and not by its *object*, which is both domestic and international.[4] It is defined by its international origin because it emanates from subjects of international law. International law is primarily the product of subjects' rules based in custom and treaty but also of their unilateral acts fitting in with the legal framework defined to this effect, and with the many practices and discourses with their variably mandatory character. The main object of this system of law is still to govern international relations among subjects of international society. But its object is no longer exclusively international. It is no longer solely the law governing relations between states (inter-state relations) or other subjects of international law, nor is it the law of international society alone. It is a system of law that aims to govern both internal and international relations and circumstances.

When international law governs relations among the subjects of international law – mostly states and international organisations (IOs) – this is the classical object of this system of law and the one that is most immediately obvious. It is usual to include in it the major areas of international law, which are those that receive most coverage, such as diplomatic privileges and immunities, the use of force and peacekeeping, the international responsibility of the subjects of international law or the rules governing IOs and especially the United Nations. It also governs a whole set of relations among states, less directly related to the vital interests of states or to the UN and which correspond to much more mundane and often more technical areas of international law, such as extradition

---

[4] See J. Combacau and S. Sur, *Droit international public*, 8th edn, Paris: Montchrestien, 2008, pp. 15 ff.

or the management and use of certain resources and means of communication. However, it must be observed that the rules and practices of international origin more frequently have as their object the condition and relations of private individuals and legal entities within states, and no longer just relations between states themselves. These new areas include human rights, labour law, environmental law, international criminal law, banking law, and also administrative law, constitutional law or part of investment law. International law applies to virtually all existing domestic and international domains and is changing exponentially in this direction, because of the constantly growing requirements of the subjects and actors of international law. This is resulting in a convergence of national systems of law through the domestic application of international norms, with national systems becoming progressively harmonised and reformed by the same rules of international origin. We are therefore witnessing the emergence of a law of international origin that is both common and internal to states.

The international legal order and internal legal orders

A legal order may be defined in several ways, particularly in sociological terms, normative terms or again in combined terms. For the time being, we shall use just a normative definition of the legal order and therefore the fact that the international legal order is a coordinated set of international norms whereas internal orders are coordinated sets of internal norms. This standard classification differentiates international law from internal systems of law by emphasising the latter's specific characters as legal orders, autonomy and self-coherence. The classification also raises a classical problem for jurists – the relations between internal orders and the international order – to which various responses are given in practice and in doctrine.

There is still a habit of opposing a monist and dualist vision of the international order and of internal orders. By the monist vision, the two types of order together form a single comprehensive legal order in which either the primacy of the international order or the primacy of internal orders is asserted. By the dualist vision, they form separate and self-contained units. This distinction between internal and international orders also leads to a differentiation in the rationales underpinning each of them. Internal, state-based legal orders are often presented as having a pyramid-like hierarchy with the constitution as the ultimate norm. This hierarchy refers to the sociological fact that internal subjects are subjected to the power of the state. Even if this presentation is oversimplified, it is still relevant to an overall understanding of how legal norms and practices are to be articulated internally. In contradistinction, the international legal order is described as a non-hierarchical set of practices and rules wherein treaties, customs, unilateral acts of states and IOs cohabit, with no explicit solution as to how they can be made compatible but with a differentiation between primary and secondary rules. Primary rules are intended to prescribe models of behaviour for the subjects of international law, and they make up the most part of international law, whereas secondary rules are procedural rules bearing on the primary rules, and provide for the way in which primary rules are made, abolished and amended. The interplay of these primary and secondary rules is essential to the proper working of international law as a legal order, but even so, currently no true hierarchy can be found among the norms, principles and practices of the primary and secondary tiers, so that a simple bilateral treaty between states is considered as having the same legal value as a general custom binding all the states in the world. This logic of equivalence among rules and the way those rules are made reflects the 'anarchic' character specific to international society. It reflects the sociological circumstances of international society in which there is no world government (the UN Security Council is not one) and states remain both sovereign and equal. Those states, as may be necessary, draw up rules or engage in practices that are merely juxtaposed. This is what may be called a 'multicentric' society by contrast with centralised domestic societies, and we can see in international law the expression of this multicentric power structure.

The internal and international orders are thus classically dissociated although, in truth, this separation is progressively fading nowadays. First, many of the rules considered to be internal are international in their origin. A growing number of international treaties, concerted acts, principles, directives, resolutions or regulations are creating obligations for national legislatures or having almost direct effects in municipal law, and most of the time take precedence over internal statutes. Next, and even if its importance should not be overstated, there is a significant development of transnational legal regimes among professionals which are increasingly autonomous, such as the *lex sportiva* for sport, the *lex mercatoria* for transnational trade among private economic actors or the *lex informatica* for the regulation of the Internet. These go beyond the two-way internal order/international order split, and give rise to what are virtually 'third-way' legal orders that are neither internal nor international. This is why the regulation of the Internet is covered only by self-regulation in the absence of any existing international rules, for want of agreement among states on this subject and in the face of the powerlessness of internal legal systems to address the issue on their own. Likewise, sports law is transnational because it is developed not by states but by international sporting federations or organisations like the International Olympic Committee. Its purpose is to govern with binding force the behaviour of professional sportsmen and women, and it can give rise to appeals to the Court of Arbitration for Sport. Finally, it should more generally be acknowledged nowadays that there are many tiers of rules of various characters and origins where the rules of international law interconnect, interweave or overlap with regional, transnational and domestic rules to encompass the same object or the same activity, whether internal or international. In other words, ours is an age of normative and institutional legal pluralism, to the extent that, for example, a European Union (EU) citizen may be simultaneously subject to rules from her internal national order, regional legal orders (like the EU and the European Convention on Human Rights) and certain world legal orders like the UN or the World Trade Organization (WTO); to which may also be added the many rules of transnational origin arising from, say, the legal regulation of trade or of the Internet. So, the common vision of a single legal order per social order must be replaced by the idea that a single legal order may govern several separate social orders, or that a single social order may be subject to multiple legal orders. This novel situation can be attributed to the post-Cold War sociological fact that the state has been weakened, to the globalisation and regionalisation of phenomena, and to the considerable development of rules accompanying these changes.

Now, the essential point here is to understand that all these elements converge gradually and interact to engender a degree of porosity between legal systems, erode the distinction between internal and international legal orders, and weaken the classical divide between internal and external sovereignty on which classical inter-state international law was built. Besides, it is no coincidence that some commentators ignore traditional concepts such as legal order in order to investigate a reality that is still difficult to perceive in its full scope. They use a new conceptual apparatus to better formulate legal relations that are being forged between the internal and international tiers. An example is the concept of legal 'space' that contrasts with the concept of a national legal order. A legal space is not associated with a particular territory. Its boundaries are shifting, and its rules and practices interweave and overlap with those of national legal orders and other legal spaces. The areas of health and safety law or environment law provide a good example of this, as do the various regional laws that are becoming increasingly autonomous. In the same way, recourse is had to the concepts of networks, flow paths and data streams when discussing rules and regulations, sometimes drawn up in a hybrid way by the subjects of international law and by private actors, themselves organised into networks that are neither classically formed international law nor internal law and which are not halted, or barely so, by state boundaries.

ASAQ is typical of this development: it is a new medication against malaria, a disease that kills more than a million people per year in the poorest countries. It was launched on 1 March 2007, is sold at a dollar a box and is unpatented thanks to an extremely dynamic network of public and private actors – including non-governmental organisations (NGOs), private foundations, pharmaceutical laboratories, public universities and UN agencies – that comply with a totally hybrid network of rules entangled with internal and international, public and private rules.

Public international law and private international law

The international law we have just defined by the international origin of its rules and practices is often characterised as *public* international law, as opposed to *private* international law. Indeed this book is about public international law, even if the public/private distinction is also fading nowadays. In contrast with public international law, private international law is composed mostly of rules of internal, state law and not of rules of international origin. It is designed to govern relations of a different type from international or internal relations: these are cross-state relations, relations between private individuals or legal entities belonging to different states. Private international law consists in applying to a given situation, for example, a sales agreement between two people of different nationalities, the municipal law of one of the two; and settling the choice of court or tribunal that will have to adjudicate any disputes over the sale. It is therefore a system of internal law that governs private cross-state relations between individuals and especially private economic actors. However, here again these definitions and distinctions between private and public international law have been eroded over several years. A dual movement is taking shape in which public international law is becoming privatised in some areas and vice versa, private international law is becoming public. In the first instance, it can be shown for example to what extent inter-state commercial disputes in the WTO merely reflect the settlement of private economic interests.[5] In the second case, one might mention the existence of ever more rules of public international law framing these relations governed also by internal law. This is the case for the rules set out by the Brussels Convention of 27 September 1968 on the jurisdiction of the courts of Member States of the European Community, the Convention of Rome of 19 June 1980 on contractual obligations or the International Centre for Settlement of Investment Disputes (ICSID) Convention of 18 March 1965.

III. Subjects and norms

At the same time, the main building bricks that make up the international legal order have also changed. We move here to a perception of the international legal order understood both as a social reality and as a normative order and, for the sake

---

[5] See H. Ruiz-Fabri, 'La juridictionnalisation du règlement des litiges economiques entre Etats', (2003) 3 *Revue de l'Arbitrage*, p. 897.

of simplification, we shall deal only with subjects and norms as the main components of this order. It can be observed that the current heterogeneity characteristic of international law is related largely to the growing diversification of its subjects and norms, and that this phenomenon throws up many questions.

Subjects

Traditionally a distinction is drawn between the *actors*, who play a part on the international stage, and the *subjects* of international law who are actors endowed with personality in international law; that is, they have rights and obligations under international law. The current change reveals that ever more actors of internal and international relations are tending to become subjects of international law, a sign of the growing amenability to law of international society.

The state

The state is the first subject of international law and the subject whose existence depends on the conjunction of a number of points of fact (territory, population, effective and independent government) that international law merely acknowledges. As such, the state is the original subject of international law. The number of states has grown substantially since the Second World War, particularly as a result of decolonisation and post-Cold War developments. There are now 193, all members of the United Nations, as against 51 that convened in San Francisco in 1945 to adopt the Charter founding the UN. Yet the state is now weakened as an actor in international relations and faces competition with the emergence of other actors and subjects of international law. Many commentators have examined the economic and political decline of the state with the latest episode of globalisation. The importance taken on by the market and certain economic and financial operators compared to states is probably the most obvious reflection of this because it seems to reduce the state's range of independent action so much. At this stage it is worth noticing above all the concomitant fact of the decline of the state's 'legal power',[6] either because states are increasingly constrained legally by IOs – on a regional scale such as the EU and on the world scale such as the WTO – or because they face competition from other producers of norms and other legal orders of a private or cross-national order, who hold sway at the expense of state's international legislative power. Likewise, international courts and tribunals have gained power to the point of engendering an international third power that has increasing influence over states, which is the logical outcome of an international society that continuously sees the hold of law increasing everywhere and is becoming increasingly complex and technical.[7] The more international law extends, the more legal regimes multiply, and resort to the courts (both international and national) increases to settle questions relating to the interpretation and application

---

[6] See J.-B. Auby, *La globalisation, le droit et l'Etat*, 2nd edn, Paris: LGDJ, Lextenso éditions, 2010, p. 136.

[7] See E. Jouannet, 'L'indépendance et l'impartialité des juridictions internationales: l'émergence d'un tiers pouvoir international?' in H. Ruiz-Fabri and J.-M. Sorel (eds.), *L'Indépendance et l'impartialité des juridictions internationales*, Paris: Pedone, 2010, pp. 135–78.

of rules. Moreover, the waning power of the state as an actor and subject of international law correlates with the formation of networks of cities, regions, experts, judges and domestic parliamentary representatives or central bank directors which create unofficial but very real spheres of power and sometimes elicit new legal practices. A significant example is the Basel Committee for banking control, made up of representatives of independent central banks of thirteen countries and which adopts minimum standards for prudential control. The upshot is that states' legal powers are watered down internationally and replaced by the emergence of myriad unofficial power centres that supplement, constrain or ring-fence the legal action and competence of states.[8]

It ensues that the state now coexists alongside other actors of international law with very varied legal standing. The phenomenon is not new in itself. Individuals and also international institutions, multinational firms, NGOs, trades unions and national liberation movements have long managed to impose themselves on the international arena and benefited from certain rules of international law, whether institutional or normative. But a dual phenomenon is observed today: the facts that these increasingly numerous and influential actors are now competing with states in the performance of certain legal prerogatives, and also that they are tending to become full subjects of international law. That is, they are the direct holders of rights and obligations by virtue of international law, and sometimes have genuine international capacities.

---

[8] For a thorough examination of these phenomena, see A.-M. Slaughter, *A new world order*, Princeton University Press, 2004, pp. 36 ff.

The other actors and subjects of international law

In the classical concept, only those who both create the rules and are the addressees of the rules can be subjects of international law, as those physical persons or juristic entities who do not necessarily create international rules but who can be the addressees of them cannot be subjects of law. The consequence of this restrictive classical definition is that it only takes as subjects of law those states and IOs that create the norms of international law, to the exclusion of all other persons or entities without that capacity. This obsolete definition, which is a legal construction dating from two centuries ago, is not in line with the hard facts of life in international law. Current legal practice shows on the contrary that international law explicitly or implicitly recognises subjects with very varied legal standing, without them necessarily having the capacity to create the rules of international law or having sovereignty, the legal attribute that still characterises the state and maintains it as an essential subject of international law. It is regrettable that some observers have not acknowledged this contemporary change and still defend an extremely restrictive conception of a subject of law that is not to be found in municipal systems.

Three main categories of actors and subjects of international law can be identified other than sovereign states and endowed with variable degrees of legal personality and capacity: (1) IOs and other public institutional actors; (2) private economic actors; and (3) civic actors.[9] IOs and international

---

[9] A distinction proposed by M. Delmas Marty in *Les forces imaginantes du droit (III). La refondations des pouvoirs*, Paris: Le Seuil, 2007, p. 137.

public actors other than states exercise the most directly visible power on the international stage, and mostly have the standing of derived subjects of international law because they are created with the agreement of states. Their rights, obligations and various capacities depend on what is provided for in their charters but incontrovertibly make them real subjects of law, the number of which is constantly increasing internationally and whose decisions, acts, directives or resolutions now have recognised effects in the internal order. Historically, the earliest IOs appeared in the late nineteenth century and became more important in the inter-war years with the International Labour Organisation (ILO) and the League of Nations. But they largely developed after 1945 with the spread of international cooperation. They currently run to several hundreds and usually have real normative and/or functional capacities, supplementing or competing with each other in terms of power and influence regionally, sub-regionally and worldwide. The best known and most significant example of this development is the 'United Nations family' which includes the UN's six main organs,[10] but also a particularly large group of related organisations, specialised institutions, subsidiary organs, secretariats and other funds.

Immediately following these public-sector actors are the private economic actors, because they have taken on growing importance with the latest episode of neoliberal

---

[10] The General Assembly, the Security Council, the International Court of Justice, the Trusteeship Council, the Economic and Social Council and the Secretariat.

globalisation, which has itself been enshrined by international texts and notably UN General Assembly resolutions. The triple movement of liberalisation, privatisation and economic and financial deregulation which these resolutions confirmed in the early 1990s reflects the new deal of the post-Cold War world, the preponderance of economic actors and especially the inescapable involvement of the major multinational firms. These multinationals benefit incontrovertibly today from a certain international legal personality, and in particular an international capacity to enter into agreements with states and also to enjoy *locus standi* in international arbitral justice – as evidenced by the activity of ICSID whose arbitration awards have constantly increased since the end of the Cold War.

Finally, the role of civic actors should be underscored, and the fact that not only are they very active internationally but they are also gradually becoming subjects of international law. In truth, while the associations, foundations, trades unions and above all NGOs are playing an increasingly important part in helping to formulate and apply international rules, especially for humanitarian law or social, human and environmental development law, for the most part they still remain subjects of internal law with limited legal capacity internationally. On the other hand, individuals themselves increasingly enjoy international rights directly, especially rights of the person, which make them into genuine subjects of international law. With the inflexible distinction established by classical international law between internal and external sovereignty, the individual was relegated in the eighteenth century to the internal sphere of states, subject to their municipal law alone. When

41

contemplated in the international arena, individuals were seen as objects of international law benefiting only from certain special or specific measures provided for by states in some domain or other. This was the case, for instance, of foreigners, refugees, soldiers on active duty, colonised individuals (the 'indigenous'), women or workers, who were the subject of certain specific international treaties but were not thought of as direct beneficiaries of the treaty rules which were binding on states alone. All this changed progressively after the Second World War, and the change has accelerated with the end of the Cold War. Universal or regional instruments have multiplied and recognise not only direct rights of individuals but sometimes certain competences too, especially in judicial matters. Besides, the most telling development in classical international law may be precisely this point: the fact that the human person is becoming a full subject of international law. This will be seen later when addressing the question of the rights of the human person as a new fundamental area of contemporary international law.

That said, for the time being this movement and its consequences have not been radical. Contrary to what certain observers were predicting at the end of the Cold War when speaking of the disappearance of states (and therefore of classical inter-state law), since the turn of the century we have seen a paradoxical resistance of the state in the international arena, especially in conjunction with security issues. So much so that, while the state is weakened and diminished in its sovereignty, especially in its capacity to formulate, control and make decisions, it continues to exercise certain legal competences (personal, territorial and universal) both internally and internationally that are crucial in legally framing the activity of other public, economic and civic actors, whether directly or indirectly.

The stakes are high because beyond the aspects of legal technique, this change raises ethical and political issues. Although all-powerful sovereign states have rightly been considered a threat to peace and the guarantee of the rights of their own citizens, and sovereignty has therefore become more functional and subordinate to the realisation of humane and pacific ends, contemporary excessive weakening of sovereignty is feared nowadays both for international peace, because weakened states are sources of instability, but also for the protection of individuals. Moreover, in the current state of international law and society, which recognises no world government nor any real world constitution (the United Nations Charter is not one), the application of certain rules of international origin (which may sometimes be of dubious legitimacy and lawfulness through, for example, WTO law or Security Council resolutions) makes it essential that the sovereign people and therefore the state can still limit the effect of such rules in the domestic order.

Norms

The rules and practices of international law also experience repercussions from the changes just mentioned. They are more diversified and far more numerous than before, and reflect new legal rationales. They increase exponentially while uncertainty grows about their normative character and their scope.

Diversification of rules, appearance of new legal practices

Rules are more diversified because different forms of amenability to law have emerged. True, the classical modes of formation of law and international law that result from them (treaties, customs, unilateral acts, general principles of law, case law) fully remain at the present time and maintain a central position in the dense legal mesh of rules and practices of international law. Their own importance has varied with the times and with the balance of power within international society. Currently, custom holds an eminent place in the international arena that is unknown to national law. Moreover, treaties remain the primary instruments of states, unilateral acts from IOs or states have never been so numerous, and case law is logically gaining influence with the rise of international courts and tribunals. But there are also a growing number of other normative instruments reflecting the development of the social and technical purposes of international law and the importance of the part played by private actors. International law has become a 'social technique' for intervention (see below) and accordingly international rules and practices are changing and new forms emerging. Where once classical international law included a small number of more formal and general rules of treaty and custom which were readily identifiable in the form of laws and duties of states, contemporary international law since 1945 and especially since 1990 includes an apparently heterogeneous cluster of material norms and practices of all kinds. This is attested to, for example, by the practice of standards like the regulatory standards developed by the International Standards

Organization (ISO), the codes of conduct adopted in the world of business, the technique of the memorandum of agreement between national regulators, the multiple declarations at the end of summits with their almost precise figures, the guiding principles like those of the OECD or guidelines such as those of the Basel Committee for coping with emergency situations in international banking crises.

These new legal rules and practices generally exhibit five characteristics:

(1) They do not usually have the same mandatory character as the classical norms of international law such as custom or international treaties; that is, they are considered to be less binding legally. They form what might be characterised as 'soft' law as opposed to 'hard' law. The limited mandatory character of these new practices and rules prompts a recurrent discussion among internationalists who disagree on whether they can really be thought of as law. This is a debate that refers everyone back to their cultural vision of what law is, in which we find the familiar divides on these issues between Continental and Anglo-Saxon legal views but also the world's North/South divide.

(2) They are composed of prospective rules and incentives rather than sanctions. In this respect, the consensus of the various actors concerned in its development or implementation is sought, and not just the consensus of states.

(3) They are far more mobile, variable and shifting. They are the immediate reflections of different substantive, cultural, social and economic objectives of international actors. They reflect a social consensus achieved among them at

a given time and in response to needs relating to a given social and political condition. They are generally rules that are renegotiated and may evolve very rapidly.

(4) They often take on hybrid forms or at least are shaped and implemented by public and private actors. They combine the joint contributions from the state and the market, from the public and private sectors, as with questions of new technologies, money, finance, trade and development but also health, employment, migration and the environment.

(5) Lastly, it is rather revealing that texts including these rules or reflecting these practices tend to grow in length as the rules and practices become more detailed, exhaustive and technical, and include an increasing amount of numerical data.

All told, these practices of international law appear to obey a new logic. They reflect the ambition to be rid of an overly rigid, excessively formal or dogmatic conception of law and to have a concrete, specialised or regionalised law adapted to specific objectives and particular contexts. The opposition is often between a law of straightforward control, supposedly related to new forms of amenability to law in which international law is simply the vehicle for the interests of certain groups of actors of international society, and a regulatory law supposedly the expression of classical international law, in which law is the vehicle for the collective interest that states have well understood.

This latest dichotomy between control and regulation is in fact rather artificial with respect to more complex existing practice. At the very least, it has the merit of nuancing the picture we have painted and emphasising that alongside these new forms of 'control' there are indeed traditional forms of 'regulation'. There is even nowadays a legal trend that runs directly counter to the simple 'multi-negotiated' mobile control just described. It corresponds to a whole series of rules and general principles that tend towards universality and the general interest, and reflect the ambition to reach a common meaning, shared by all the actors and subjects of international relations. Examples of this might be the rights of the human person, the fundamental prohibitions laid down by international criminal law on the crime of genocide, war crimes or crimes against humanity, the prohibition of the use of force or the legal principles related to sustainable development. As a result, we find in the international arena this inevitable dichotomy – which runs through any society when it becomes increasingly law-based – between social (instrumental) functions of law and its normative (universal) functions, between the usages of law that depend on the specific interests and the characteristics of generality and universality which are often attributed to it to achieve common principles. Repercussions of this dichotomy can be seen on the various forms of amenability to law that make up the international legal order.

The increased number of legal rules and practices
The legal rules and practices of contemporary international law are also growing impressively in number. The output of this multiform, classical and new, hard and soft, prescriptive and incitative system of law meets ever-increasing needs from social actors. This quantitative increase in laws also arises from the fact that in international law, more than in municipal law,

very few existing texts are abolished. Treaties, directives, resolutions and declarations follow one another without the advent of new rules being offset by the loss of existing ones, since obsolescence or lapse are always under discussion. New legal practices multiply while new customs are created, new treaties are adopted and unilateral acts proliferate. We are faced with a previously unknown situation of 'pan-legalism' in international terms, in stark contrast to what classical international law has been.

This multiplication of the number of classical and new rules of all kinds and of different scope renews the question of their normative character, their perception/representation, and their effectiveness and their legitimacy. In an international society that remains polycentric but also diverse and pluralistic in terms of its actors, activities and centres of interest, in which universal institutions are at risk of becoming unproductive by the multiplication of their tasks, the law that is produced is the subject of manifold challenges.

It is to be feared, first of all, that the inflation of new practices might distort the legal realm and make the boundaries between law and non-law uncertain, contrary to the requirements of predictability and stability that are often sought through the legal rule. This is what was meant by Prosper Weil's famous criticism made some years ago.[11] Against that criticism, it is perfectly possible to defend soft law and new forms of legality – as I myself do. However, the difficulties must not be overlooked. Moreover, the increased number

---

[11] P. Weil, 'Towards relative normativity in international law?' (1983) 77 *AJIL* 413 ff.

of rules of all kinds undermines their credibility. Law begins to produce uncertainty and knowledge of it becomes problematic. This results in a dangerous opacity. There is a real threat that ordinary citizens, although often the subject matter and sometimes even rights holders in international law, will have no understanding of it. They are powerless in the face of incomprehensible international regulation which is perceived by some as oppressive. The invasive presence of international law in municipal legal systems is considered by part of the world to be legal imperialism, having been achieved by a situation of unequal constraint where the international commitment of their state to abide by these rules has often been merely a front obtained under economic and political duress. But the question of the representation of international law is far more general, because it also affects all of the new and old international actors, including states themselves. A shared feeling may emerge that it is impossible to assimilate the proliferation of rules accompanying the purposes of contemporary international law (see Chapter 3, section I). The position of experts and professionals of law is then reinforced, but without any cause for rejoicing. It fails to solve the problem of representation and accessibility to rules by other actors – or by professionals themselves for that matter – and that merely intensifies the idea that knowledge is confiscated by an elite, which deprives the rules of their legitimacy. The problem is no longer one of drawing up and applying rules but that their drawing up and application is guided by so-called experts claiming to have true knowledge. There is a danger here of unlimited and diffuse social control being exercised because norms are produced by those holding knowledge and power rather than democratically.

But that is not all. As legal rules and practices multiply in all domains, by the same token they may be losing their effectiveness. They are far more vulnerable, open to criticism and subject to malfunctions. There is a risk that they are more fragile as they develop, because this accumulation in volume threatens their full enforcement. They encompass too many domains for them to regulate properly. Instances of violation and circumvention of the rules posited, exceptions and dispensations are on the increase. This in itself is a logical conclusion, but reinforces a feeling of ineffectiveness or disillusion with regard to the force of international law. The more social domains these rules and practices cover without achieving the hoped-for result, and the more of them that accumulate to solve a given problem without being really effective, then the more disillusionment or even resentment they create among those who are their objects or subjects. Let us take a detailed example to size up the problem. Article 25 of the Universal Declaration of Human Rights provides that 'everyone has the right to a[n adequate] standard of living'. Article 11 of the 1966 Covenant on Economic, Social and Cultural Rights speaks of 'the fundamental right of everyone to be free from hunger'. The Vienna Declaration and Programme of Action adopted in 1993 by the World Conference on Human Rights emphasised that extreme poverty and social exclusion are violations of human dignity. The Copenhagen Declaration on Social Development and the World Summit Programme of Action for Social Development in March 1995, the latest World Summit on Sustainable Development held in Rio in June 2012 and the Declaration adopted in February 2005 on the tenth anniversary of the World Summit for Social

Development reasserted, for this reason, that the fight against extreme poverty should remain a high priority for the international community. Objectives of the fight against extreme poverty were set in the context of the Millennium Declaration adopted in 2000 by the UN General Assembly. The Resolution on Human Rights and Extreme Poverty, which has been adopted each year by the UN Human Rights Commission, aims at connecting the issue of extreme poverty with that of the indivisibility of rights and raises the problem of the poorest not exercising their civil and political rights.

However, extreme poverty is a phenomenon that still affects a billion people who survive on incomes below the vital minimum of a dollar per day. What, then, is the point of these many international declarations and texts? The current phenomenon of 'pan-legalism', by which increasing numbers of domains are subjected to the practices and discourse of international law or are framed by it, creates the dangerous illusion that any problem in international law can be given a seemingly legal answer, whereas sometimes ethical, social or economic answers are needed. The international norm, whether soft or hard, is asked to control everything, to regulate everything, but because law cannot satisfy everything, this may ultimately make it partially ineffective, devalued and delegitimised.

IV. Unity or fragmentation

Because of these developments, another question concerning the present-day international legal order is posed with particular acuity: the question of whether it forms a true order or whether, on the contrary, it is on course to breaking up irremediably into many different orders. It is more specifically a question of the unity of the international legal order. There must be some unifying or coordinating principles governing these rules and practices for the order to constitute an ordered set and not just a mere cluster of disparate components. Thus, the existence of the international legal order depends on the existence of a minimum principle of unity or coherence, and this is currently a problematic issue.

Review of the factual and doctrinal situation

We have seen that the distinction between internal legal orders and the international legal order is tending to fade in part, that the sovereign state still exists although enfeebled and facing competition from other subjects of law, and more generally that we are up against a situation of strong legal pluralism, a situation that classical international law did not encounter, at least in this form. In a sense, the phenomenon of legal pluralism in the international arena is as old as international law itself, because it is an order that never had either a centre or an apex and which, ever since it first emerged in modern times in the eighteenth century, has had as its vocation to govern multiple and non-homogeneous states. Besides, the question of the unity/fragmentation of international law is not a new one at all and has perplexed jurists since the nineteenth century. However, it cannot be denied that this phenomenon has taken on unsuspected scope nowadays, and that the growing lack of homogeneity among the norms of international law and the multiplicity of the legal practices and regimes adopted are liable to raise far more concrete problems than before. The question is, what real impact does this multiplication of rules and practices, subjects and power centres have on the possible unity of the international legal order and therefore on its very existence as an order? Is the international legal order breaking up and therefore seeing its own identity diluted as international law, or is it moving towards a new order that is becoming unified and coherently coordinated to become a global system of law? Or again is there just one international law that breaks into multiple branches, or are we witnessing the emergence of several international/regional/cross-national legal systems with no connection between them?

Let us review things. Contemporary international society is becoming a society of law characterised not by the form of a world state which does not exist and never has existed, but by a set of institutions and of 'provinces of law';[12] that is, regimes of legal rules and different practices coexisting in comparative indifference to each other. The international legal order is divided in order to respect the particularity of the different social and economic activities now devolved to it, and because each of the subsets of norms, institutions and legal practices adopted provides specific responses and fulfils a function aimed at satisfying a specific need. In other words, these subsets are necessary for international law to fulfil its many purposes but they promote a segmentation of the subject matter to the detriment of the major units; they give the image of an international law that is ever more divided and disorderly among the many legal regimes such as those relating

---

[12] The expression 'foyers de droit' is taken from J. Chevalier, *L'Etat postmoderne*, Paris: LGDJ, 2004, p. 94.

to human rights, environmental law, economic law, European law, and so on. With the latest episode of globalisation, it may even be thought that international law is continuously being disarticulated because of the increasing overlap of international, cross-national or private normative spaces that abide by their own cohesive principles. At the same time, once again, this vision cannot be overstated because alongside this continuous division certain principles tend to be recognised as superior and common to all of the regimes and international law. The result is that the current legal reality is criss-crossed by opposing trends: on one side, law is divided; on the other, it holds up certain principles as being more fundamental than others (formal and material), which enjoy broad consensus and which, as such, can tend to introduce coherence or even a degree of unity at a global level.[13]

Contemporary international law appears to be a strange conjunction of forces of attraction trying to form a common whole, and repulsive forces trying to maintain independent parts. It seems to be torn between unity and plurality, between universalism and cultures, between globalisation and regionalisation, between constitutionalisation and fragmentation, between the rights of states and the rights of individuals, between the law of public actors and the law of private actors. These forces are many and draw the international order into a process of increasing heterogeneity. They are paradoxical because they seem to oppose each other: does not the universalism of the rights of the person stand against the relativism of

---

[13] See P.-M. Dupuy, 'L'unité de l'ordre juridique international. Cours général de droit international public', (2002) 297 *Recueil des Cours*.

the diversity of cultural expressions? The clauses of company law against free trade agreements? Does the globalisation of certain principles not run counter to the regionalisation of certain legal regimes? Does not a possible constitutionalisation of law under the aegis of the United Nations Charter run counter to the fragmentation of this law into multiple sets of rules? And what of the law of states against human rights? These forces are strange in that they resist the logic that might be expected of them in a classical scheme. They depict a vision of international law that cannot be represented by the metaphor of the decentralised circle of classical international law or the centralised pyramid of internal orders. The impetus of these various forces is compelling current international law to progress in a disorderly and unpredictable way. It branches off in several places, at the crossroads of several legal regimes which coexist indifferently, without any rank order, to such an extent that it now seems to be more of a hotchpotch than a system.[14]

In the wake of this evolution, new divisions have arisen in contemporary doctrine of international law which give a different interpretation of these developments. Since the Second World War, the idea of progress, which was at the core of classical internationalist thought, has been called into question by the bad habits of the internationalist past. The benchmarks laid down by the great doctrinal edifices have disappeared and there are no more predetermined answers that can impose themselves with certainty. We are witnessing a proliferation of approaches and doctrines that seem to reflect the

---

[14] See J. Combacau, 'Le droit international: bric-à-brac ou système?' (1986) XXXI *APD*, pp. 76–85.

disarticulation of classical international law. For the purposes of presentation, they can be arranged into two opposing camps. On the one side, there are postmodern ideas of irreducible pluralism which see in the disorderly evolution of international law the proof of its irreversible fragmentation and the proven impossibility of its rationalisation and unification. On the other side, there are the ideas that maintain the principle of unity or at least of a certain coherence in the international legal order, which they interpret differently:

- through doctrines of complexity in which the international order remains a coherent legal order but a complex one with heterogeneous elements in a state of tension which can only be resorbed in the form, say, of 'ordered pluralism' respecting plurality;[15]
- through doctrines of world governance which convey the notion that these sets of rules, networks and new legal practices reflect the emergence of a new form of regulation of international society associating public and private actors, official and unofficial powers in a permanent negotiation;
- through doctrines of constitutionalisation of the international legal order, in which multiple sets of rules are subsumed under fundamental common principles that take precedence over other rules and set up a founding hierarchy of an order in the course of constitutionalisation (especially via the United Nations Charter or human rights).

---

[15] See M. Delmas-Marty, *Les forces imaginantes du droit (II)*. *Le pluralisme ordonné*, Paris: Le Seuil, 2006.

An order in the process of growing complexity: the existence of tangled hierarchies

The debate is far from over. The fact is that the existence of international law as a legal order depends on one or more principles of unity or autonomy which have to be proved and may be of different natures: material or formal, organic or mechanical, hierarchical or circular, static or dynamic. Here we cannot discuss the possible existence of all these principles, so we shall settle for simply observing that current international law is akin to a complex legal order, in line with a process corresponding to the inevitable proliferation of all our contemporary legal orders. In truth, at first sight it is rather the 'disorder of normative orders' which seems to define contemporary law and to replace the old order of classical international law articulated around sovereign states alone and their statutory outputs (their rights and duties).[16] But this disorder is less the reflection of a total legal anarchy of existing legal regimes than it is the translation of a system of law that is growing increasingly complex. This complexity means that it is made up of manifold and heterogeneous components that feed back to varying extents into each other and which are both antagonistic and complementary. It is notably made up of 'tangled hierarchies'[17] that

[16] See N. Walker 'Au-delà des conflits de compétence et des structures fondamentales: cartographie du désordre global des ordres normatifs', in H. Ruiz-Fabri and M. Rosenfeld (eds.), *Repenser le constitutionalisme à l'âge de la mondialisation et de la privatisation*, Paris: Société de Législation Comparée, 2011, pp. 45 ff.

[17] See F. Ost and M. Van de Kerchove, *De la pyramide au réseau? Pour une théorie dialectique du droit*, Brussels: Publications des facultés universitaires de Saint-Louis, 2002, p. 14.

obey internal and external feedback processes formed within each legal regime (e.g. within human rights, environmental law, European law, etc.) and between the regimes themselves (e.g. between the regime of human rights and the regime of the environment and European or South American regional law, etc.). In this we identify not some meta-principle of hierarchy but several features of hierarchies that are neither unique, nor centralised, nor fully coordinated. They generate many small (very partial) pyramids of norms, which are interpreted differently within each regime and may migrate from one regime to another, or even sometimes impose themselves to some extent on all regimes. These factors may also provoke tension or conflict, or even be radically opposed. The existence of these separate and tangled hierarchies is confirmed by the presence, which is common within each normative unit, of a power of control or even sanction that interprets the higher principles and aims to ensure they are upheld more or less effectively, diffusely and autonomously. Lastly, this complexity is also due to the structure of international power which, as seen, is diffuse, non-homogeneous and distributed among official seats of power that may be in competition with each other (states and IOs) and unofficial seats of power that may unilaterally impose their decisions on official seats (markets, lobbies, multinationals, NGOs).

The legal effects of the different components of the hierarchy vary with the specialised legal (human rights, environmental law, trade law, etc.), regional (European law, African law, etc.) or worldwide (UN, ILO, WTO, etc.) regimes which accommodate those effects but without any clear coordination. For example, Security Council resolutions under

Chapter VII of the UN Charter (peacekeeping) are binding on all UN members and take precedence over their treaty commitments by the interplay of art. 103 of the Charter (ICJ orders of 14 April 1992 after the Lockerbie air incident). Conversely, UN resolutions do not necessarily prevail within regional legal orders (see the cases of Ahmed Ali Yusuf and Yassin Abdullah Kadi tried by the Grand Chamber of the European Court of Justice, 3 September 2008). The principles of *ius cogens* also introduce hierarchical factors. Initially enshrined in arts. 53 and 64 of the 1969 Vienna Convention on the Law of Treaties, *ius cogens* has been extended to many other areas and now has a more general scope. It is defined as a small group of mandatory principles, considered so important for the international community that it is impossible to depart from them in any way. A *ius cogens* rule cannot be transgressed and takes precedence over any other material international and even cross-national rule (*World Duty Free* v. *Kenya Award*, ICSID, 4 October 2006). In this way, the prohibition of genocide was characterised as a rule of *ius cogens* by the ICJ in a ruling of 3 February 2006 (case of armed activities in the territory of the Congo). Likewise, the prohibition of torture has also been recognised as a norm of *ius cogens* by several courts and tribunals, and is considered to prevail over any other practice or substantive rule contrary to it (*Prosecutor* v. *Anto Furundzija*, ICTY, 10 December 1998; *Al-Adsani* v. *UK*, ECHR, 20 November 2001 and *Bayarri* v. *Argentina*, IACHR, 30 October 2008). Clearly in this case the *ius cogens* rule introduces a normative hierarchy on a world and regional level, based on ultimate respect for the dignity and integrity of the human person.

Lastly, one also sees emerging hierarchical legal elements related to the existence of general principles of law. These are bound up with a legal regime, whether a functional (general principles of the law of the environment), regional (fundamental principles of EU law) or worldwide (principles of the UN Charter) legal regime, and it has to be observed that they are increasingly used nowadays precisely because of the constant expansion of international law and its subdivision into several sets of rules. However, the fact that these general principles have attained a pre-eminent or at least an essential position within the various existing legal regimes actually has ambivalent effects on the question of unity/fragmentation. On the one side, these principles may reflect a tendency towards unity because of their common use by various legal regimes. Each general principle introduces hierarchical tendencies into a given legal regime: principles of community law, European law, human rights, environment law, international trade, and so on. But some of these legal principles migrate from one legal regime to another, from a functional regime to a regional or worldwide regime and vice versa. For example, we might cite the general principles of procedural law, dispute settlement or treaty law as good faith or *pacta sunt servanda* ('agreements are to be kept'), respect for human dignity or the elementary principles of humanity. Some principles which seem very specific to one regime, such as the precautionary principle for the environment, may also migrate towards other regimes, in the case in point the regime for healthcare law. This is also the case for the principle of equal treatment formerly arising from economic law, found again in the law of international public service. The principle of humanity itself was formulated for the first time in humanitarian law in the celebrated Martens clause of the 1899 Hague Convention and now tends to move into other regimes. The principle of non-discrimination arising from human rights is now common to almost all regimes. While originally arising from a specific regime, these legal principles introduce coherence into the global order, or even a low degree of hierarchy into the entire order, because they are called on to restore unity in these different units or at least to coordinate them around a few basic axioms. The result is that the consolidation of special and regional regimes through their own general principles is no impediment to the possible internationalisation of principles common to regimes and the global order, nor to the introduction of a hierarchy in favour of this global order. It is a sign of the progressive harmonisation of their foundations while respecting the pluralism of each. In other words, the conclusion at this stage would be that the general principles are pushing in the direction of unity or rather harmonisation of the system, and not towards its fragmentation.

However, if we stopped at that the review would be too partial and would omit other elements that cast a more nuanced light on this question. The general principles, in fact, exert a more ambivalent influence on the legal order than was foreseen. On the other hand, it must be understood that this influence cannot be fully grasped unless allowance is made for the political interplay of international actors/subjects, because everything depends on the choices made by those actors in favour of some principle or other. The actors can thus take advantage of the many uncertainties and contradictions that affect the general principles to support their political strategies, and use them to shore up the autonomy of a legal regime and its indifference to others (tendency to fragmentation), or, on the contrary, to harmonise their legal regime with another (tendency to coherence and unity). As a result, different policies of resort to these principles are outlined by the different international courts and tribunals, the leaders of organisations or by states, which vary in their interpretation on this subject and tip the scales in favour of fragmentation or unity.

International law is currently subject to multiple developments which are causing its crisis of identity and a need for redefinition. Some of its classical representations or definitions have become oversimplified with respect to international and domestic reality which has grown far more complex. International law is the product of subjects/actors whose conduct it is designed to govern. It must be understood in terms of feedback with this social substrate, which has changed with the latest episode of globalisation. From this perspective, using the concept of legal order to describe contemporary international law entails deliberate simplification and formalisation. The concept of an international legal order is a convenient instrument for simplifying the presentation of international law. To continue to be useful, the international legal order must be understood in a broad and inclusive sense. It must not be severed from its shifting sociological background, and any idea of the different legal orders being separated from each other must be abandoned. International law can no longer be defined as an ordered, autonomous and logical arrangement of its various components, but much more as a network of processes and sets of rules, discourses and practices that do not have simple linear relations but rather relations characterised

by migrations, partial hierarchies and feedback loops, in which
the former logic of classical international law, ordered around
a sovereign state and its output of statute law, sits alongside the
new rationales associated with the emergence of new actors
and subjects. International law is ultimately a tangle of rules,
practices and regimes reflecting order and disorder at one and
the same time.[18]

[18] On these possible entanglements, see M. Van de Kerchove and F. Ost, *Le
système juridique entre ordre et désordre*, Paris: Presses Universitaires de
France, 1988.

3

International law as an instrument of regulation and social intervention

We have seen that international law is a historical culture, which arose from European thought and has been disseminated worldwide. We have also seen that nowadays it forms a legal order open to transformations that break up the classical categories into which it used to be arranged, casting doubt on its very existence as an order and creating an identity crisis. It remains for us therefore to consider international law in terms of its purposes and its main areas of application. Like any other system of law, international law is ordered around certain purposes which are its reason for being. Like most national systems in today's societies, international law aims to achieve these purposes by exercising increasingly diverse functions, which go beyond its primordial and classical function of regulating conduct and managing conflicts. Without being able to list all of those functions in the framework of this book, I would like above all to show that it has become a law of regulation and intervention, and that in this double objective, which has been conferred on it by its social environment, lies one of the main explanations for the changes underway. This is what shall be outlined first (section I) before studying what today seem to be the three fundamental pillars of its area of regulation and intervention, namely peace (section II), development (section III) and human rights (section IV).

I. End-purposes

To say that contemporary international law is about both regulation and intervention means that it has become a fully liberal-welfarist law. Contemporary international law obeys a double liberal and welfarist purpose, which to a large extent explains its current extension into a regulatory and interventionist form. It is used both to manage problems of peace, coexistence and cooperation among states, and also to safeguard the well-being of the world's population. Its objective is to govern the world of states and international actors, but also the lives of individuals and peoples, their rights and freedoms, their health and their education. It has not just a role of regulating international relations but it is also an instrument for intervening within national societies and international society. The one explaining the other, it is these purposes/functions of international law that explain the developments observed in Chapter 2. These functions emerged and expanded with the new international context when international society became a post-colonial and post-Cold War society.

The liberal end-purpose of international law

The liberal aim of regulating coexistence and also cooperation among states and other actors and subjects of international law is easy to identify because it is the legacy of classical international law. It is ordered entirely around principles of respect for state sovereignty, personality, equality among states and neutrality with regard to internal political regimes characterised by the celebrated principle of non-interference in a state's internal affairs. It is the subject of more than three-quarters of the provisions of the United Nations Charter. It therefore remains an essential component of contemporary international law based on the classical representation of an international society in which states are still considered to play a crucial part.

Besides, as has been pointed out several times, the era of decolonisation, which was a major event of the twentieth century and seemed to overturn the bases of the older international order, was paradoxically a period when the classical liberal dimension of international law was reinforced. This was attested to, for example, by Resolution 2625 of 24 October 1970 (Declaration on the Principles of International Law concerning Friendly Relations and Cooperation among States) which was emblematic of the time, and sets out the principle of equal sovereignty among states as fundamental:

(a) States are juridically equal;
(b) Each State enjoys the rights inherent in full sovereignty;
(c) Each State has the duty to respect the personality of other States;
(d) The territorial integrity and political independence of the State are inviolable;
(e) Each State has the right freely to choose and develop its political, social, economic and cultural systems;
(f) Each State has the duty to comply fully and in good faith with its international obligations and to live in peace with other States.[1]

---

[1] Text available at http://daccess-dds-ny.un.org/doc/RESOLUTION/GEN/ NR0/348/90/IMG/NR034890.pdf?OpenElement.

There could be no clearer reaffirmation of the fundamental principles of the liberal aspect of classical international
law, and especially the principle of equality among states and
the neutrality of international law with regard to the forms of
states' political and economic regimes. It is easy to understand
the force of attraction and the power of seduction of the classical liberalism of Western origin for an international society
which, in 1970, was in the process of decolonisation and in
which international law was extending to all the world's states.
Up until decolonisation, international law was a stigmatising
law in itself, which merely reflected the imbalance of power
among states, the feeling of the superior civilisation of a whole
political class and the racism of an age. International law itself
was an instrument of denial of recognition and of domination,
because it was based entirely on the fundamental discrimination between civilised and uncivilised states. So, after decolonisation, the recognition of equal status for all through the wider
application of classical liberal law supremely manifested the
recognition of the identity and equal dignity of new states.
This recognition of status, which put an end to the discrimination of the colonial period, did not lie in the affirmation of
a right to be different but of a right to equality that ignored
differences and that is indeed indifferent to differences. This
was compounded by the principles of neutrality and respect
for pluralism that allowed new states to coexist, introducing
much more heterogeneity. Also reasserted were the specific
features of the liberal objective of classical international law:
the personality of the state, therefore its standing as an individual subject of law; its inherent rights which from that point
on it could not be stripped of, and again the principle of free

choice and therefore of the reassertion of the will of the state as the foremost expression of its sovereignty.

This classical liberal aim of international law, consolidated in 1945 and reasserted in the 1970s, has not vanished with the advent of the latest episode of globalisation, but it has now found alongside it a welfarist aim that has gained in scope as never before.

The welfarist end-purpose of international law

The welfarist objective is as old as the liberal objective but it was not really materialised till the inter-war years and especially after 1945. Just as liberal states in Europe became welfare states at the end of the Second World War, contemporary international law developed into interventionist welfarist law brought to bear on international society and national societies so as to offset their human, economic, social and cultural imbalances.

From 1941, the freedom from need and the well-being of individuals were set out as features of future international peace. In the Atlantic Charter, US President F. D. Roosevelt and UK Prime Minister Winston Churchill included these as future objectives of international society (points 5 and 6), by affording 'assurance that *all the men in all the lands* may live out their lives in freedom from fear and want'.[2] The objective was to fight internationally the evils that their democracies experienced internally during the inter-war years, in particular

---

[2] Text available at www.un.org/en/aboutun/history/atlantic_charter.shtml. Emphasis added.

unemployment and ignorance to which they attributed the rise of fascism and Nazism in Europe. The ideals of well-being and the fight against poverty were to be directly included as purposes to be accomplished in art. 1(3) of the United Nations Charter: 'To achieve international co-operation in solving international problems of an economic, social, cultural or humanitarian character.'

UN Charter art. 55 further specifies this provision of article 1 and grounds all UN action in economic and social matters by setting out the explicit objective of 'the creation of conditions' of 'well-being'. Institutionally, a special organ, the Economic and Social Council (Ecosoc, art. 61) was set up. It was to become one of the main organs of the UN and operated the major welfarist objectives. In normative terms, the welfarist aim of international law threw up a whole array of legal practices that ranked alongside those of the liberal purpose of classical regulation. The most characteristic features and the main difficulties can be outlined briefly.

First, this welfarist law is very much a law of intervention and not of abstention or mere regulation. By that I mean that it reflects a legal interventionism in the broad sense of the term by states that affected a large number of areas of individual experience and therefore spread as a humanistic, social and welfarist law. The welfarist dimension of contemporary law therefore intrudes far more into the internal affairs of states as it seeks directly to ensure the happiness and well-being of individuals and peoples within their own states. This largely explains why present-day international law has become as much a law of internal relations as a law of international relations.

Second, the welfarist material objective, and not the formal liberal one, is almost unlimited in its area of application and intervention because there is no real limit to the desire to be free from need and risk. These are not readily commensurable needs, with the result that they fuel potentially indefinite demand internally and internationally.[3] The list of domains in which the UN intervenes could not be more instructive in this respect as it covers almost all areas of the lives of individuals. The Repertory of Practice of United Nations Organs indicates the following as 'practices' of the UN: engendering institutional and normative law, standards of living, full employment, economic development, natural resources, the world supply of food, international trade and finance, transport and communication, population matters, migration, social welfare, narcotics, cartography, cooperation on cultural matters, education, the fight against disease, and so on.[4] The Millennium Declaration adopted by the General Assembly in 2000 added as its priority objectives the reduction of poverty, the promotion of gender equality and empowerment of women, primary education for all, a sustainable environment, the reduction of child mortality, improvement of maternal health, the fight against HIV/AIDS and malaria, the right to health, the right of access to medicinal drugs, protection of vulnerable groups (children, the elderly and disabled) but also everything relating to the internal transformation of states by the imposition of the principles

---

[3] We take up the analyses of Pierre Rosanvallon here because the analogy with present-day international law is striking: P. Rosanvallon, *La crise de l'Etat-providence*, Paris: Le Seuil, 1992, pp. 33 ff.

[4] *Repertory of practice of United Nations organs*, 1956, vol. III, pp. 3 ff.

of the rule of law, good governance, democracy and human rights.[5]

Third, the welfarist objective of contemporary international law relies as much upon private practices and private actors as on public ones. The development of welfare law is accompanied by multiple forms of amenability to law described earlier in which 'public' international regulation now stands alongside private and negotiated multicentric legal practice, which increasingly escapes the control of the bureaucratic apparatus of international institutions and states. This welfare law is deployed increasingly via a tangled web of 'public' and 'private' services and by networks and interrelations between traditional public actors, civic actors and private operators. This has developed further with the new post-Cold War consensus and the latest episode of globalisation. It might be thought that a welfarist and social law could not spread in a world that was very largely subjected to neoliberal globalisation of the economy, but the fact is that legal practices of welfare law can be perfectly supported by today's globalised liberal practices, from which they sometimes seem divorced. They can be achieved equally through a private contract or through a public multilateral treaty, and they may involve private actors as much as public ones. An example might be the implementation of the Kyoto Protocol, adopted on 11 December 1997, the purpose of which is part of an ultimately welfarist and interventionist logic because it is about ensuring the survival of the population and even of the planet by limiting world pollution through the reduction of greenhouse gases. The

---

[5] www.un.org/millennium/declaration/ares552e.htm.

71

Kyoto Protocol was adopted by states and seems to depend on states alone. But that is just an appearance: the private sector is very largely mobilised to ensure the actual implementation of the Protocol through private companies, in the context of the Protocol's two flexibility mechanisms: the 'clean' development mechanism and joint implementation. Private companies in industrialised countries are directly concerned with investing in 'clean projects' within developing countries or with trading carbon quotas within 'transitional' economies such as Russia or Ukraine.

Fourth, contemporary welfarist international law is public policy law and meets an ever-widening need for security. Here we find the impact of a far more global development of internal societies which are progressively becoming 'risk-sharing' societies.[6] International society itself is now comparable to what Jürgen Habermas calls an 'involuntary risk society' in which states are forced to act together to confront global or cross-national risks such as criminal trafficking of all kinds, terrorism, ecological risks, pandemics or economic and financial crises.[7] It is striking to see to what extent international actors increasingly perceive economic, social, environmental or humanitarian problems as global *threats* to international security. This new perception has direct consequences on the legal characterisation of certain facts and, from that, on the

---

[6] See U. Beck, *La société du risque. Sur la voie d'une autre modernité*, Paris: Flammarion, Champs, 2001, pp. 35–6.

[7] J. Habermas, *Le projet de paix perpétuelle. Le bicentenaire*, Paris: Le Cerf, 1995, p. 74. 'Kant's idea of perpetual peace: At two hundred years' historical remove', in Habermas, *The inclusion of the other*, Ciaran Cronin and Pablo de Greiff (eds.), Cambridge, Mass.: MIT Press, 1998, 165–202.

legal regime that is deduced from it or the actions that are decided. To take the world and UN example, one might cite the way in which the UN Security Council now characterises certain economic, humanitarian and social problems as being 'threats to peace' in the same way as wars or conflicts are threats. This new type of characterisation was originally theorised by a group of experts of various nationalities, the High-Level Panel on Threats, Challenges and Change, which was put in place at the request of the UN Secretary-General. In 2004, the Panel produced a report which UN Secretary-General Kofi Annan presented publicly at the UN. The Report deliberately placed 'Economic and social threats, including poverty, infectious diseases and environmental degradation' at the head of six clusters of threats with which it claimed 'the world must be concerned now and in the decades ahead'.[8] But the principle of security is found more generally on many levels and in very many areas, with the result that it provides the basis for many present-day legal texts or at least accounts for their adoption. For example, in the WHO context, there is talk of 'global public health security' to confront the risk arising from human behaviour, climate change, infectious diseases or natural catastrophes;[9] in the context of the IMF, of 'financial security'; the ILO and 'employment security' or 'social security'; in the context of the 1990 Convention on Migrant Workers of 'security of migration flows', and so on. In a similar way, the United Nations Development Programme (UNDP) recommended some years ago

---

[8] *Report of 1 December 2004. A more secure world: our shared responsiblity* A/59/565, p. 12.
[9] www.greenfacts.org/en/global-public-health-threats/index.htm.

the creation of an 'Economic *Security* Council', different from the now side-lined Ecosoc, as the counterpart to the Security Council tasked with peacekeeping. The new council would have had as its objective world economic and social security, and would have had to set up and coordinate 'the broad policy framework for all global development issues. These issues range from food security to ecological security, from humanitarian assistance to development assistance, from debt relief to social development, from drug control to international migration.'[10]

We are therefore witnessing two closely correlated phenomena: on the one hand the concept of security has been constantly expanding since the last episode of globalisation, and on the other hand it is becoming a factor of acceleration of the practices and principles of welfarist law. International law is called on to respond to all of these new risks and collective threats: it steers the way in which individuals, populations and states order their lives, because the life of each is considered from now on as a risk factor for others. Accordingly, such a development reinforces the point that welfarist international law is indeed 'public policy' law (*loi de police*) in the sense given to the term in the great treatises of the eighteenth century; that is, its purpose was to make 'civilised' (*policé*) the conduct of states and individuals in such a way that they should live harmoniously together in well-being and complete security. However, the extension of such double-acting (national and international) public policy law is not at all neutral and

---

[10] UNDP, *Human development report 1992*, New York, Oxford: Oxford University Press, 1992, p. 79.

prompts reflection on the possible transformation of international society into a police society and the emergence both internationally and internally of a 'biopolitics' – in the sense given to the term by Michel Foucault for national societies – that is, an international policy focused more on life than on liberty. Without considering that we have reached the stage of a control society, we are witnessing the emergence of a multiplication of rules which tend increasingly to deal with the body, health, eating habits and housing practices, living conditions, space as a whole, the existence of the world population. All of the space extending from the organic to the biological and from the individual body to the population tends to be taken in hand, regulated and disciplined through this welfarist law. Out of concern for the security and well-being of this huge social body that is formed by the world population, institutions, agencies, states and NGOs are now introducing the premises of massive control of social forces. This contains the seed of a benevolent paternalism that aims to do good for populations without necessarily taking account of their free opinion, by identifying populations more as assemblies to be regulated than as peoples free to govern themselves.

However, care is required in analysing these developments because the positive aspects of this welfarist law should not be overlooked. This law is also the instrument of a more social, equitable and solidarist law, focused on individuals and peoples and not on states. But it is important to remain watchful of its effects because the predominance of a welfarist law may engender legal and political excesses which would eventually be of particular concern for those same individuals and peoples.

A liberal-welfarist international law

Lastly, it should be emphasised that international law has not become a strictly welfarist law for all that, but it is indeed a liberal-welfarist law and in that lies one of the ultimate keys to its identity crisis and its existence as a legal order. The fact that it is, at one and the same time, a liberal and a welfarist law means that there is dialogue between its two aims and therefore between its functions of regulation and intervention. In other words, international law is a law characterised by antagonistic and complementary purposes and functions, each with its own logic.[11] It is not the outcome of a harmonious synthesis among them; it is made up of the competing and complementary array of many legal regimes which those two objectives engender in what remains an unresolved state of tension. This tension explains the diversity, the recurrent oscillation and the possible contradiction between the relevant legal tasks, practices and discourses. It makes it possible to understand certain paradoxes of contemporary international law and of its unpredictability. It also explains one of the sources of the contestation and attraction of international law. Despite the very fierce criticism regularly levelled at it, international law combines in its two objectives the intersecting and varied expectations of one and all, because its liberal dimension reflects respect for all forms of freedom and sovereignty while its welfarist dimension can attenuate the economic and social risks that the exercise of freedom and sovereignty might create.

[11] See E. Morin, *Penser l'Europe*, Paris: Gallimard, 1987, p. 28 and *Introduction à la pensée complexe*, Paris: Edition Sociale Française, 1990, p. 99.

Now, it is by bearing in mind this dialogue-like tension between these two essential purposes and functions of contemporary international law that it is proposed to examine three of its areas of application which seem the most fundamental and representative. They are not chosen at random but correspond to the purposes set out in art. 1 of the United Nations Charter and were reiterated as such by the UN General Assembly at the 2005 World Summit: (1) maintaining international peace through the obligation of peaceful settlement of disputes and the introduction of a collective security system; (2) development of states, especially by means of economic and social cooperation; (3) human rights. These are the three pillars represented by peace, development and human rights, and they should ensure for individuals 'freedom from want, freedom from fear and freedom to live in dignity'.[12] As can be seen, they form a triptych which is closely related to the immediate circumstances of the post-war world, but which is just as topical not only because of the UN action along these lines but also because of their incontrovertible value for the subjects of international law and their considerable normative development. These three pillars are also particularly interesting because they form the main lines of contemporary international law and what could be the architecture of a new pacified (peace), equitable (development) and humanistic (human rights) world society. They form a normative horizon that is both strong and coherent but which we already know requires legal and social interventionism for certain peoples

---

[12] Report of UN Secretary-General Kofi Annan, *In larger freedom: towards development, security and human rights for all*, 2005. A/59/2005.

and which, it shall also be seen, is not without debatable effects in each of the three areas concerned.

II. The first pillar – peace

Modern international law of the eighteenth century arose largely out of the law of war. This was the focus of many European jurisconsults of the law of nations and notably the famous Dutch jurist, Hugo Grotius, who has long been presented as the father of international law with the publication of his *De Bello ac Pacis* in 1625. As seen in Chapter 1, the international law on the use of force was for a very long time one of the most important and codified domains of classical international law. The break with this system occurred only in the aftermath of the Second World War.

The United Nations Charter

After the early attempts to set up a collective security system with the League of Nations and the prohibition of the use of force in the 1928 Briand–Kellog Pact, it was the United Nations Charter of 1946 that made the right to use force unlawful by having as its fundamental objective, at the end of two world wars, 'to save succeeding generations from the scourge of war, which twice in our lifetime has brought untold sorrow to mankind' (Preamble). Peace was enshrined as the first goal of the United Nations, and the originality of contemporary international law after 1945 has been to make the prohibition of the use of armed force the new fundamental principle of international relations. According to the observation of the US representative in San Francisco, at the Conference at which the Charter was negotiated, the intentions of the authors of the original text were to declare an absolute and unrestricted ban in the most general terms.[13] This principle was solemnly affirmed in art. 2(4) of the Charter but it can only be properly understood if construed with the other provisions of the Charter and particularly with arts. 2(3), 51 and 42. Through the interplay of these different provisions, the drafters of the Charter sought to build a genuine legal regime of law against force (*ius contra bellum*).[14]

Immediately before art. 2(4), art. 2(3) lays down a general obligation for the peaceful settlement of disputes as the necessary corollary of the prohibition of the use of force. This principle must therefore supersede the old one because previously recourse to war was not only accepted but considered as a perfectly legitimate means (even if controlled and limited) of settling international disputes. The obligation to settle disputes peacefully is now the only lawful means of satisfying opposing claims between states in the international arena, and in this respect international law proposes a whole array of means ranging from simple diplomatic negotiations between states to the use of an international court or tribunal via good offices, mediation or reconciliation. Articles 1(1) and 42 of Chapter VII of the Charter provide for the substitution of a collective security mechanism for the old individual law of the

---

[13] UNCIO, vol. 6, p. 335.
[14] See O. Corten, *The law against war. The prohibition on the use of force in contemporary international law*, Oxford: Hart Publishing, 2010.

use of force. The essential idea is that in the event of the use of force or the threat of infringement of peace in breach of the prohibition posited by art. 2(4), the United Nations would itself prevent the dissident state from acting, if necessary by using armed force (Chapter VII, art. 42). It is international collective action, referred to as collective security or policing and not war, that is triggered and placed under the authority of the Security Council. However, the drafters of the Charter were already aware, notably with respect to the experience of the League of Nations, of the possible limits of any collective security action. They therefore maintained the old right of each state to use force individually to ensure its self-defence in the event of armed attack (art. 51). In other words, the 1945 Charter does mark a major turning point in contemporary international law by imposing a general ban on the use of armed force, but this principle suffers exceptions of various kinds: one exception, benefiting each state, with the individual right to defend itself recognised for any sovereign state if another state attacks it militarily, and another exception, in the common interest of all, with armed collective security action under the aegis of the Security Council in the event of an infringement or threat of infringement of international peace and security.

Contemporary practice

The entire mechanism has been the subject of evolving contemporary practice, especially since the end of the Cold War and raises questions about its possible changes. Three remarks can be made on this issue.

Changes in the use of force today

First, it should be pointed out that the system put in place in 1945 did not put an end to the unlawful use of armed force. We have witnessed a marked rise in the number of internal – and often internationalised – conflicts, such as in Africa or the destabilisation of many states after the end of the Cold War. Different groups (governmental or otherwise) unlawfully use armed force against their own populations. Moreover, some states have claimed a right to intervene militarily in another state for humanitarian reasons even if the Security Council has refused them that right. Whatever the validity of their moral arguments, they therefore make unlawful use of force. This is what happened with NATO's intervention in Kosovo in 1999 and that of the United States (and its allies) in Iraq in 2003, both of which were carried out in breach of international law. Lastly, art. 51 has been invoked controversially on several occasions and has been the subject of lively discussions of interpretation among states to determine, in particular after the terrorist attacks of 11 September 2001, whether a state (the United States in the case in point) could engage in pre-emptive self-defence in the event of a mere threat of armed attack. This claim was denied by a clear majority of states but it is indicative of attempts to circumvent the article. In view of the various possible instances, it can be seen that the prohibition in art. 2(4) falls foul of a patent lack of effectiveness and efficaciousness, and that the palliatives provided for in Chapter VII and art. 2(3) clearly exhibit their limits in the face of the repeated determination of certain states to get around them. They are not entirely ineffective, and this does not challenge

the actual existence of the rule on the prohibition of the use
of force as a treaty-based and customary rule binding all states
(*Military and Paramilitary Activities in and against Nicaragua*,
ICJ, decision of 27 June 1986), but it attests to the difficulties
in enforcing it in a contemporary world that remains riddled
by multiple tensions and in which national and international
societies still remain largely conflict-ridden (democracies included).

Second, the current multiplication of the number of
international armed actions, this time lawful ones, should be
highlighted, together with the change in their purpose. The
new international consensus achieved among the great powers
of the Security Council after the East/West divisions of the Cold
War has made it possible on several occasions, on the basis of
Chapter VII, to send armed forces with an offensive role to
restore or impose peace (such as in Iraq, former Yugoslavia,
Haiti, Rwanda, Somalia, Libya, Ivory Coast), which should
not be confused with the classical missions of UN troops (simple passive role of interposition or observation). These new,
post-Cold War, armed interventions have often been referred
to as humanitarian interventions because the infringements
of international stability necessitating them to be triggered
no longer correspond to the former situations of war among
states (international conflicts) but more often than not to internal conflicts or internal circumstances engendering serious
violations of rights (famine in Somalia, genocide in Rwanda,
ethnic cleansing in former Yugoslavia, brutal quelling of peaceful demonstrations in Libya). So to justify such armed interventions, the Security Council has had to interpret the terms
of Chapter VII loosely by considering that serious violations of

human rights or large-scale humanitarian tragedies adversely affect international stability.

Criticism

We are witnessing a post-Cold War reappraisal of the use of force – whether in the context of Chapter VII or in breach of it – or even a *revaluation* of this use of force when it comes to humanitarian interventions. This evolution, which corresponds in part to the importance given to human rights today (see below), elicits questioning and criticism. First, when so-called humanitarian interventions occur in violation of the UN Charter (Kosovo and the second intervention in Iraq), they are not just unlawful in the eyes of international law but are also dangerous for the future. They may create precedents that can be invoked by other states and they open up Pandora's box, threatening a return to the unilateral use of armed force. In other words, they reflect a real step backwards compared with the arrangements put in place in 1945. On this occasion, the old concept of 'just war' reappears in order to lend moral legitimacy to unlawful interventions: war is unlawful but just and therefore morally necessary to save populations. This type of justification also takes us a step backwards, because it has been seen that the modern international law of war was devised in the seventeenth and eighteenth centuries to escape from the dangers and perverse effects of the doctrine of just war. Rehabilitating just war to justify the use of force without the approval of the Security Council could take us back to a state of endemic war that modern-era jurisconsults did their utmost to escape.

Next, even when decided by the Security Council, these armed humanitarian interventions have been perceived in some areas of the world as neither more nor less than the expression of a new imperialism of the major powers, when the states at which the interventions are aimed are always weak states and never the major powers themselves or their protégés. Present-day military and/or humanitarian interventions, even of the UN type, are usually carried out on the basis of a distinction among states and more especially with respect to how their regime is classified (liberal and democratic, or not); which implies a discriminatory treatment policy, obviously perceived negatively. There follows a global representation of the world in which states are ranked according to their degree of maturity and a hierarchical system of international power is rehabilitated; a regime of double standards is therefore applied. During the 2000s, certain American and European decision-makers were seen to be reusing the idea of empire to support this new humanitarian hegemony, which raised new fears and seems particularly dismaying in view of the history of international law and the way it legitimised European domination and colonisation of three-quarters of the planet.

That posited, it must still be understood that while peace was announced as the prime purpose of the United Nations, the San Francisco negotiators did not contemplate it from the security angle alone. The aim was also to create the conditions for successful economic and social development of all the world's states. Development has thus become a dominant paradigm of the contemporary world, closely related to the idea of international peace but also to the whole past history of international law and the current idea of international social justice; and it also drives a constantly evolving legal practice.

III. The second pillar – development

Classical development law

Development is another major domain of contemporary international law, in institutional and normative terms. In the immediate aftermath of the Second World War and especially with the decolonisation of the 1950s and 1960s, development was contemplated as a possible key to the reconciliation of post-colonial society and an instrument for achieving greater international justice. It was considered a means to end inequality in the distribution of wealth between formerly colonised states and formerly colonising states, the former being thought of as poor and underdeveloped but as being capable of quickly making up the gap to the latter, thought of as rich and developed states and presented as models for development.

The development paradigm

Articles 1(3) and 55(a) of the UN Charter clearly include development among the objectives for the new post-war international legal order, with art. 55(a) even using the term 'development':[15]

---

[15] See A. Pellet, 'Commentaire de l'article 55, alinéas a et b', in J.-P. Cot, A. Pellet and M. Forteau (eds.), *La Charte des Nations Unies. Commentaire article par article*, Paris: Economica, 2005, p. 1453.

> With a view to the creation of conditions of stability and
> well-being which are necessary for peaceful and friendly
> relations among nations . . . the United Nations shall
> promote:
> a. higher standards of living, full employment, and
>   conditions of economic and social progress and
>   *development*; [Emphasis added]

The idea of making development an objective of the United
Nations was not unanimously held at the time, far from it.
The USSR was a priori keenly opposed to it, because it feared
that respect for state sovereignty and the principle of non-
interference might be infringed using the pretext of development policy. It therefore wanted the UN Charter to be confined
to the single objective of international peace and security. But
it was ultimately the American and British positions of Roosevelt and Churchill that prevailed. These went beyond the sole
issues of maintaining security and extended to the successful
economic and social development of all states worldwide as
a springboard for securing peace. Development was included
in the Charter as one of the foremost ways of ensuring world
peace in the long run. This subordination of development to
peace was to be criticised on the ground that it was rather peace
that should be in the service of development. Nonetheless, the
principle of development is now hard set and has met with
favour, through the decolonisation of the 1950s and 1960s, that
the drafters of the Charter had not dared imagine. With this
decisive impetus, art. 55(a) becomes the real legal basis of what
has been called the 'development ideology' within the United
Nations.

Through this change, the UN has evolved into a major centre of aid for underdeveloped countries. It named the 1960s the 'Development Decade', suggesting that (then-termed) Third World countries would be developed in ten years' time thanks to the legal and economic policies and rules of development. The first legal rules of technical assistance, transfer of resources and aid were put in place both in the context of IOs and through bilateral or regional treaties. Besides, apart from conflict-ridden situations relating to certain independence movements, the former colonial nations said they were ready to help the new states, just as were the two major powers in the post-war world (the USSR and US), which were clearly anti-colonialist. From the 1950s onwards, the northern countries constantly proclaimed their readiness to help the development of the southern countries, and they eventually conceded certain derogatory and preferential regimes in favour of the South. In fact, these legal concessions were limited in several ways and were only to be accepted by Western countries because they were persuaded they would remain at the centre stage of the new post-colonial society. Such a paternalistic and hegemonic vision was consolidated by the fact that the global model of economic development taken up by the newly independent states did not entail any direct challenge to the worldwide liberal economic and financial system put in place after the Second World War with the GATT, the IMF and the World Bank.[16]

---

[16] The Bretton Woods Conference led to agreements signed on 2 July 1944 on the creation of the IMF and the International Bank for Reconstruction and Development (IBRD or World Bank). The GATT

Two points are worth noticing. First, the political and humanistic aspect of development was left aside, leaving the focus entirely on the question of economic development. The two major powers agreed to decouple the economic side of development from its political side, which was entirely consistent with the aspirations of the young Third World nations eager to maintain their national sovereignty above all; this was to become one of the characteristics of classical international development law. Second, the new legal practices concerning the development of poor states were presented as replacements for the old European imperialist system and were based on a new vision of the world in which all states were equal. Where classical international law had once established a hierarchical type of relation between colonised peoples or protectorates and colonising or protector states, post-colonial international law placed all states of 'the development era' on an equal legal footing with the same rights and duties. Unilateral constraint and the colonial system of exploitation were superseded by the idea of international cooperation enabling nations to undergo a change in condition from underdeveloped to developed. This economic and technological development was presented as a solution which had the advantage of going beyond ideological divides, because it was evaluated on the basis of scientific, economic figures that were supposedly neutral and objective, and not on the debatable subjective values of a particular civilisation. Now, the decolonisation movement of the 1950s and

signed on 30 October 1947 came into force in 1948. Together they form the basis of the institutional and normative framework of the liberal international economic system of the post-war period.

1960s, based on the right of peoples to self-determination that was hailed as a new principle of international law, seems to have reinforced this vision, because it gave all formerly 'uncivilised' peoples access to independence and put them on an equal legal standing with the former 'guardian' states.

In point of fact, appearances are partially deceptive because the concept of development is far from being neutral and reflects, as is known, one of the most fundamental beliefs of the West.[17] Development is merely the continuation in another form of the old idea of progress that had been largely discredited after 1945. Above all it restored certainties to an age rocked by the Second World War. Yet, the issue of development was not spawned by decolonisation but above all by the concerns of European industrial states in the nineteenth century which went on to colonise half of the planet. Development was initially a concern of rich countries and not poor ones, of the colonising and not the colonised or decolonised countries. The development of the latter was appraised with respect to the developed state of the former. This is why the decolonised states were immediately characterised as 'underdeveloped', then by the more diplomatic term of 'developing countries'. There resulted an inevitable and unusual continuity between the international legal discourse and practice before 1945 and the discourse and practice of international development law. States were ranked on a scale according to their level of development, and the pairing 'underdeveloped'/'developed' nations maintained South/North relations

17   See G. Rist, *Le développement. Histoire d'une croyance occidentale*, 3rd edn, Paris: Presses de Sciences Po, 2007.

in a dichotomy based on a difference in circumstances between the two, with the same persistent idea of a possible transition of the country lagging behind to the position of being a frontrunner and of serving as a model for the stragglers. So just like the work of colonisation/civilisation before, development was presented as highly positive, desirable and necessary, and it served as justification for all of the legal rules adopted along these lines. In short, development was the continuation of the policy of Western colonial domination by other means, and this original aspect marks it to the present day as intrinsically ambivalent. It was only with the current success of the major emerging states that the feeling of pride and self-esteem seems to have become a reality for some of them, not because this success breaks the devaluing symbolic structure of the development ladder and what it presupposes, but because at least those states now find themselves at the top of the ladder, and they are perhaps changing world society into a post-Western society.

The evolution of classical international development law

The expression 'international development law' (*droit international du développement*) was introduced in the 1960s by French internationalists.[18] Several of them brought together and systematised a whole set of rules and legal practices under this

---

[18] The principle of international development law was introduced in France by André Philip, at a conference in Nice on 27–9 May 1965: *L'Adaptation de l'ONU au monde d'aujourd'hui*, Paris: Pedone, 1965, pp. 129 ff. It was taken up by Michel Virally in 'Vers un droit international du développement', (1965) *AFDI*, pp. 3–12.

new term. In this way they sought to show that a new branch of international law had emerged for the benefit of developing countries that was autonomous with respect to other legal branches and could be the subject of separate teaching and research. This development law was composed mainly of dual norms, a function of the material difference in the circumstances of states, with some rules relating to developed countries and others to relations between developed and developing countries. Although it was the subject of much criticism, international development law did indeed emerge at the time as a set of legal rules and practices designed to meet the aspirations of many developing countries, to solve their development problems and by doing so to remedy the glaring socio-economic inequalities between states in the aftermath of decolonisation.

Institutionally, what is sometimes called the 'United Nations system for development' has been put in place, with the creation of several organisms like the UNDP and the United Nations Organisation for Industrial Development (UNOID) prompting considerable deployment of international bureaucracy and expertise in the service of technical assistance operations – financial aid being in the hands of the IMF and the World Bank. In terms of rules, international development law rests on a small group of fundamental legal principles such as permanent sovereignty over natural resources, the free choice of economic system and the principle of equity. It also corresponds to a set of more technical rules of an interventionist, discriminatory or preferential character. They differ from ordinary rules of international law applicable to other states when they try to correct the failings of the existing liberal legal and economic system by making up the gap in the material situations between developed and developing states. One can cite especially the transfer of resources, technologies and knowledge from rich to poor countries, preferential regimes and the famous enabling clause in favour of poor countries introduced in the GATT, which allows these countries to benefit from a derogatory and advantageous system in commercial terms, the tentative agreements on basic products, or the principle of common but differentiated obligations in domains relating to the seabed and the environment. This set of principles and rules was reasserted in the 1960s and 1970s within a New International Economic Order (NIEO) which Third World countries hoped would supersede the existing legal and economic order. Proclaimed by simple UN General Assembly resolutions (see especially GA Resolution 3281 of 12 December 1974), the NIEO sought to bring about a wholesale reform of the international order, in particular of international economic law, so as to offset the extreme economic and social imbalance in post-colonial society and to introduce social justice among states.

But this impetus for legal reform was broken in the 1980s for many reasons, both internal and external to decolonised states, leaving the arena to the prevailing neoliberal model within post-Cold War globalisation. This reflected the implementation – via the normative actions and instruments of the IMF and the World Bank, but also General Assembly resolutions – of a triple movement of deregulation, privatisation and liberalisation of all economies and financial and monetary markets that buried any idea of NIEO and applied the same neoliberal model of development to states, rich or poor, worldwide.

In truth, despite the incontrovertible impact of neoliberal globalisation, there still remain today many legal practices relating to the specific economic development of the poorest states (classical development law) whereas new rules and practices were adopted after the Cold War and correspond to a new understanding of development, the high point of which is without contest the concept of sustainable development.

The law on sustainable development: a new model of development and a new system of law

In 1992 the UN believed that for the first time worldwide it had produced a renewed and common vision of development, especially with the Agenda 21 adopted in Rio. This new vision reflected a multidimensional understanding of development that had been unknown until then but also, and more profoundly still, a new way to envision and protect the future of humankind by revising our ways of living, producing and consuming. The new development model runs counter to economistic reductionism induced by ultra-liberal globalisation. It extends well beyond the classical development model to encompass a whole array of practices and principles in the service of new ends (human, social and environmental) while having a global dimension, concerning North and South at the same time which it had not previously contained. It advocates a form of environmentally friendly development and the renewal of resources so as to preserve the planet. But it also integrates the concern to combat disparities in wealth and poverty. This form of development is characterised as 'sustainable' because, by what is now a famous expression, it must meet 'the needs of the present without compromising the ability of future generations to meet their own needs'.[19] It therefore has an intergenerational dimension which calls on the (moral) responsibility of current generations with respect to their offspring. In other terms, the sustainable development model reflects the need to respond globally and intergenerationally to the risks facing humanity. This involves a new concept of development combining sustainability in space and time, and seeking to halt the current form of economic production based on unbridled growth that increases inequality and pollutes the planet.

The law on sustainable development is the legal reflection of this new multidimensional and intergenerational model. It brings together a vast and varied array of legal principles and practices, which are more or less constraining, resulting from a series of initiatives ranging from the 1972 Stockholm Declaration on the Human Environment to the latest Earth Summit in 2012, via the Rio Declaration of June 1992 on the environment and development, Agenda 21, the many treaties adopted in this area, including the 1992 Convention on Climate Change – to which was joined the Kyoto Protocol that came into force in 2005 – but also principles and rules relating to economic, human and social development.

The 1992 Rio Earth Summit was the driving force in this domain. The principles adopted in the final Declaration and Agenda 21 founded a new law of sustainable development. The principles bring together development law and environmental law but they more generally include legal rules and

[19] *Our common future* (Bruntland Report), United Nations World Commission on Environment and Development 1987, point 27.

practices from three areas looking to reconcile the idea of sustainable development (Agenda 21, Preamble I, 1): economics (growth and production), social and human (human rights, fight against poverty and unemployment) and ecology (protecting the environment).

Implementation

Difficulties in application may, however, be found because of strains and possible contradictions arising from the three pillars – economic, social and environmental – of sustainable development. These reveal an essential basic problem today as to whether one of the rationales should prevail over the others. International financial or commercial institutions, tasked with the economic side of development, implement legal rules of an economic order promoting the liberalisation of trade and foreign private investment in poor countries, but this purely economic logic may entail pollution of the biosphere or plundering of countries' traditional know-how or natural resources. Human and social logic may prevail at the expense of ecological considerations while it is very often accompanied by criticism of the economic and financial logic, which has adverse effects for human rights and human development. The environmental logic may lead to protecting forests and natural areas, promoting renewable energies or limiting poaching of certain protected species, but sometimes this is to the detriment of the economic and social rights of the local communities and indigenous populations. Besides, opposition arises in this respect between North and South because their interests diverge when it comes to the various dimensions of sustainable development. Poor states are often concerned primarily with maintaining their economic growth to be able to develop relative to rich states, for which the environment is becoming more of a priority. As a result, as Sylvie Brunel tersely puts it, the problem is that 'the rich emphasise sustainable, but the poor still think development'.[20]

These questions of compatibility are still unanswered today other than on a case-by-case basis in line with existing legal regimes, but at the present time, the global trend is for economic interests to prevail. As set out above, contemporary international law is a juxtaposition of legal regimes adopted amid general indifference of the ones for the others and therefore with no real connection between them. The international legal order may therefore include, at one and the same time and without any specific solution for their coordination or articulation, neoliberal economic international law and legal norms of human and social sustainable development law. Each new regime is created at the whim of states and other actors of international society according to their own needs without them being overly concerned about their possible contradictory effects. It is not because there are many direct conflicts between norms from different legal regimes, which rarely occurs, but simply because there is no consideration of the norms of one regime by the subjects and actors of another that, for example, environmental or social rules cannot normally produce legal effects with regard to commercial relations organised among states under the aegis of the WTO. This is a logical outcome of the partially disordered character

[20] S. Brunel, *A qui profite le développement durable?* Paris: Larousse, 2008, p. 9.

of contemporary international law and of its lack of adequate rules of compatibility or a genuine hierarchy of norms. It is why, between the ambitious stated objectives of law relating to sustainable development and their actual achievement, there is still a gulf summarised by the final Declaration of the latest Earth Summit in Rio in June 2012. The overall results for sustainable development are very sparse and particularly disappointing, so much has the world environment degraded further and the gap between rich and poor countries persisted or even widened.[21] The purely private market and financial logic currently wins out at the expense of any general and human interest – given that the system is based entirely on the law of the market – and for the time being does not in any way solve the problems of pollution and the state of poverty in which billions of people still live.

That being the case, it should also be emphasised that, in its environmental aspect, sustainable development law very clearly enshrines the principle of two-speed legal treatment between industrialised and developing countries and so reintroduces a spirit of equity which seemed to have vanished from many areas of international law. Some legal principles of environment law are intended to commit all states, such as the principle of participation, the precautionary principle, environmental evaluation and the polluter-pays principle, but the specific circumstances of developing countries are still taken into account to diversify the obligations of all sides. For example, the entire Kyoto Protocol relies on this distinction

---

[21] Final declaration of 22 June 2012, *The future we want*, point 19 ff. www.un.org/disabilities/documents/rio20_outcome_document_complete.pdf.

by imposing legal obligations on developed states alone. Enshrinement of this two-speed treatment is sometimes legitimate for developing countries, in two ways: environmental pollution was caused by the economic activity of industrialised countries, which confers on them a particular responsibility in the area; and developing countries, for their part, need to develop industrially and so to be able to emit pollution. Furthermore, it is the weak and poor states that are most affected nowadays by climate change, because they do not have the financial or material resources to cope with it. It remains only to be seen which states are developing countries and which no longer are, because a major (so-called emerging) state like China, which has become the world's second power, can elude restrictive environmental obligations in this way.

Development and human rights

Sustainable development goes along with another equally fundamental change in international law on development. This is the ever closer connection since the 1990s between human rights and development in that all international texts, the acts of IOs, General Assembly resolutions and states' declarations henceforth associate the two. In art. 1(3), the drafters of the Charter had already grouped development and human rights as the main purposes of the United Nations, but they had subsequently been separated to be entrusted to separate organs.[22] They are now reunited again. This results in a series of significant shifts within development law. Whereas classical

---

[22] See O. de Frouville, 'Commentaire article 1, pargraphe 3', in Cot, Pellet and Forteau (eds.), *La Charte des Nations Unies*, pp. 358–9.

international development law and the NIEO were wholly focused on the classical framework of international law and respect of the sovereign freedom of the state, and whereas they advocated the principle of neutrality with regard to the political regime of developing states and their sovereign freedom as to the choice of development model, present-day development law imposes on sovereign states a particular, non-neutral model of development based on human rights, good governance and democracy. Classical and new development law are now vehicles for legal rules and practices that rely on different concepts of the role of the state and the nature of sovereignty. Indeed sovereignty is becoming functional in the context of the new model because it is subordinate to the achievement of the human ends of development. But the result is more specifically that human rights are now considered as both the means and the end of development. On the one hand, human rights are thought to contribute significantly to the country's economic development by strengthening people's free choice and potential to take initiatives – perceived as the real driving force of development as 'development agents' – with the result that human development and human rights are becoming necessary conditions for economic development. On the other hand, human rights are considered to be the ultimate objective of this new development model which is entirely ordered around human beings and no longer around states.

IV. The third pillar – human rights

This shift should not come as a surprise because it reflects a general tilting of contemporary international law in favour of human rights and the human person dating back to 1945, but which has only been reflected in practice with the end of the Cold War. While classical international law was built entirely around the sovereign state and its rights and duties, contemporary international law marks a clear change of direction to the advantage of the rights of the human person, so materialising the third pillar on which it stands, pursuant to the goals of the United Nations Charter.

Change

The new wave of liberalism of human rights and democracy which unfurled over Europe and America in 1945 had a predictable impact on the drafting of the UN Charter. The new democratic impetus is to be found in the earliest wording of the 1945 Charter which, because of the determination of the US delegation in Committee I/1 in San Francisco, was finally imposed with that concept: 'We the peoples of the United Nations.' This was an adaptation of the opening words of the US Constitution, 'We, the People of the United States.' Furthermore, the Charter was the first legally binding instrument to declare on the world stage the principle of respect for human rights (especially arts. 1(3) and 55(c)). At that precise time, the first legal marker posts of what I term the second, liberal end-purpose of international law emerged, that is, the liberalism of human rights. However, the question of human rights is addressed only partially in the Charter whereas three-quarters of its provisions concern, as said, the rights and obligations of states and the principle of non-interference in internal affairs (art. 2(7)). US President Harry Truman, who closed the

San Francisco Conference, promised to start work immediately on an 'International Bill of Rights' so as to appease the many NGOs, especially from the US, which in the face of the horrific Nazi crimes wanted to append to the UN Charter an international declaration of human rights with binding legal force. This promise was to lead to the UN member states adopting the Universal Declaration of Human Rights in Paris on 10 December 1948. The Declaration thus became the new founding text of international human rights, but even so it remains no more than a General Assembly resolution without binding force.

In the wake of the Universal Declaration, instruments guaranteeing human rights were adopted regionally in South America (1969) and Europe (1950), but it was not until more than twenty years later and the two UN Covenants of 1966 (and their entry into force ten years later) that a legally binding regime properly began to take shape worldwide. It was only with the end of the Cold War that international human rights law developed in normative and institutional terms, became stronger regionally[23] and progressively extended to many areas of classical international law. The legal discourse on human rights has now spread worldwide, if we consider the way it has swarmed into all regimes and branches of international law, the ratifications of the main international instruments on human rights, and UN actions along these lines in the last twenty years.

[23] An African Charter of Human and Peoples' Rights was adopted on 27 June 1981 in the context of the Organisation of African Unity and came into force in 1986. The African system of human rights now includes a commission and a court.

Generally, human rights have become a transverse rule of contemporary law affecting almost all areas of international law. For example, even claims relating to foreign investments and patent protection, which may seem particularly remote from these concerns, are often presented nowadays in the language of human rights.[24] However, it would take too long to review all of these areas here, and we shall confine ourselves to tracing the impact of the new legal discourse within the UN.

The 1993 Vienna World Conference revitalised human rights on the world stage. Its outcome was the adoption of a Final Resolution and a Programme of Action which reflected the rediscovered consensus of the international community in favour of human rights; throughout the Cold War years, East, West, North and South had been keenly opposed on the nature and scope of human rights. In addition, these texts called on the UN to develop its action in this area and in particular to set up an Office of the United Nations High Commissioner for Human Rights (OHCHR). The OHCHR subsequently became the main office of the United Nations tasked with promoting and protecting human rights worldwide, and the focus for new impetus in this direction. The OHCHR also aims to see that all UN organs and institutions take account of the defence of human rights in their actions. In a 1997 report on renovating the organisation, the Secretary-General confirmed this impetus and called for the generalisation within the UN of an approach founded on human rights. He asked that in

---

[24] R. Wai, 'Countering, branding, dealing, using economic social and cultural rights in and around international trade regimes', (2003) 14 *EJIL* pp. 35 ff.

future human rights be taken into account in 'each of the four substantive fields of the Secretariat's work programme (peace and security; economic and social affairs; development and cooperation; and humanitarian affairs)'.[25] This approach was indeed to be extended to all areas. Moreover, this change was not belied but on the contrary reinforced over the years, as illustrated by the new call from the UN Secretary-General in 2005 for greater integration of human rights in the UN system. In his report to the General Assembly, he recaptured the original spirit of the Charter, recalling that human rights are one of the three pillars of the UN system together with development and security (art. 1).[26] The outcome document adopted by the General Assembly to conclude the 2005 World Summit confirmed the strengthening of the UN machinery in favour of human rights, democracy and the rule of law (art. 123).

At the same time, the United Nations deployed unprecedented activity in favour of democracy and the organising of free and fair elections in many states. The results achieved are apparently satisfactory because, according to the UNDP, the number of countries having adopted the characteristics of democracy rose from 60 in 1985 to 160 in 2012. Moreover, massive violations of rights were to prompt armed intervention and humanitarian intervention missions in the territories of sovereign states: Somalia, Rwanda, Haiti, Kosovo, Iraq, Libya and Ivory Coast. As seen above, the principle of

---

[25] See *Renewing the United Nations: A Programme for Reform*, doc. A/51/950, Report of the Secretary-General 1997 (point 78). www.undg.org/docs/ 1400/Renewing_the_UN_A_Programme_for_Reform_A51_950.pdf.

[26] Report of UN Secretary-General 2005, *In larger freedom: towards development, security and human rights for all*, 2005. A/59/2005.

international action to end systematic violations of human rights and reconstruct a state in a democratic form was secured in the 1990s through a new consensus among permanent members of the Security Council and a loose interpretation of Chapter VII.

Lastly, it should be emphasised that this new legal discourse accompanied the post-Cold War development of international criminal justice and the appearance of a new branch of international law, international criminal law. The special tribunals for former Yugoslavia (1993) and Rwanda (1994), the International Criminal Court (1998) and the various hybrid criminal courts and tribunals are the expression of a clearly asserted will to put an end to the impunity of those who commit crimes against humanity (massive and systematic violations of rights), crimes of genocide (extermination of a group) and war crimes (serious infringements of the laws of war with respect to combatants and civilians).

States' rights and human rights

This international law of human rights must be set alongside the classical liberal objective of upholding states' rights. The two forms of liberalism, the classical liberalism of the rights of states and the liberalism of human rights, are both connected with liberal philosophy. It is that philosophy that underpins human rights because they are directly rooted in enlightenment philosophy and eighteenth-century Euro-American political liberalism. But it is that same philosophy that underpins the classical liberal international law of states. The classical liberal framework of international law based on equality and the sovereignty and freedom of states imposed itself because of the specific structure of multicentric European society, but also because it was constantly powered by liberal thought and its European ideological corpus. We can thus observe a double movement of emergence of rights at the same time: human rights which were an internal victory against absolutism, and the rights of states which were a victory against the Pope, the Holy Roman Emperor and any attempted domination by another state. However, these two forms of liberalism, constituted into legal arrays, can oppose each other head-on, because whereas the classical liberalism of international law is pluralistic and consecrates the principles of neutrality with respect to states' internal choices, the liberalism of human rights is non-pluralistic liberalism and not neutral. The former is based on the principle of neutrality with respect to the form of internal political regimes and the non-interference in the internal affairs of states, whereas the second aims to impose rights and liberal pluralist democracy on states. Whereas classical liberal law ensures 'formal justice' in protecting the interplay of the sovereign freedom of states, the liberalism of human rights imposes a 'substantive good' extending beyond their sovereign freedoms. In other words, the international law of human rights is not one branch of international law among others, because in the long run its introduction implies a far-reaching change within national societies. It is quite plainly about setting up the rule of law and a liberal pluralist democratic regime within national societies. It is also ultimately about human rights prevailing over the sovereign rights of states, about making individuals true subjects of international law and becoming the ultimate beneficiaries of all international law. The shift is particularly important, and the two inter-state and humanistic aims of international law may engender directly opposing legal obligations for states as subjects of law.

The concept of sovereignty is at the heart of these contradictions, because how can the intrusive intent of human rights for the sovereign state be reconciled with the classical concept of sovereign independence? Many commentators have spoken of the *splitting of sovereignty*, a split between a classical and a functional conception. The classical liberal objective of international law rests on an indeterminate conception of the sovereign freedom of states that respects the national sovereignty of states. The liberal aspect of human rights law rests on an idea of functionalised national sovereignty, organised around certain human ends it aspires to achieve and possibly leading to the introduction of the rule of law. Clearly, from the democratic liberal perspective and the human rights perspective, being a sovereign state means being a state in which the people are truly sovereign, in which power is limited and individual freedoms are observed. It is this specific conception of sovereignty which would ultimately be achieved by the state as a sovereign state, as a community of human beings who are themselves free. In this case, one can obviously no longer speak of negative formal sovereignty in the sense that it would remain entirely indeterminate, and in that the state might do whatever it wants in its internal order so long as it does not infringe the sovereignty of others. Accordingly, without necessarily putting an end to it or implying complete legal monism, without spelling the abandonment of classical principles of coexistence and cooperation, international human rights law may lead to a far-reaching transformation of the liberal goal of classical international law and of all national societies. International human rights law is also, and this cannot be overlooked, a way of preventing possible excesses of classical sovereignty leading to an oppressive domestic policy and an aggressive foreign policy. Human rights were promoted internationally in 1945 so as to attempt to prevent crimes being committed in complete impunity behind the screen of sovereignty.

Criticisms

The destiny of contemporary international law is therefore also that of human rights, which are the most crucial internal variant for the future. They open up a new front and an infinite task to be pursued. They feed democratic demand, giving rise to new requirements internationally and the refusal to settle for the existing situation imposed by force, tradition or gender. But this far-reaching transformation of contemporary international law comes in for criticism on several levels. First, it can be queried what a global society might be in which human rights would become the 'ultimate norm of all politics',[27] and the alpha and the omega of the internationalist horizon? While we can easily agree that human beings should be the highest value for the future international legal order, human rights cannot constitute the only option, trump any policy or be the key to international problems. Human rights cannot, for example, be the solution to economic and social

[27] B. Boutros-Ghali, *Secretary-General's opening address of the UN world conference on human rights*, Vienna, 14 June 1993, A/Con. 157/22.

inequalities among states. Second, the effectiveness of human rights is often called into question insofar as, outside of the regional level, legal instruments for rights are little respected, subject to many reservations and not accompanied by means of court control to compel states to meet their obligations in this area. In this respect, one might cite the Convention on the Elimination of All Forms of Discrimination Against Women (1979). The dismaying paradox is that this is one of the most widely ratified conventions in the world, yet at the same time the convention that has the most reservations by states parties. It is also often pointed out that the rights enshrined in international texts do not form a clearly identified category, increasing numbers of them having no clearly defined content, which is unlikely to clarify their implementation and their effectiveness. Lastly, one can also question the legitimacy of their content and origin by denouncing their overly Western character which makes them unsuited to other cultures in the world. This seems to be the most debated issue, and is increasingly dividing various states worldwide.

Internationally, the line of confrontation on human rights has very clearly moved since 1989, because it is now much less the question of civil and political rights versus economic and social rights that divides states, than the question of the place of culture and of cultural specificities with regard to the universalism of human rights. This shift in concerns with regard to human rights after 1989 can be explained by the end of the East/West ideological confrontation over social and political rights and the era of recognising questions of identity and culture. This requirement has been reinforced with the UN humanitarian interventions which have sometimes been badly perceived by public opinion, with new policies of conditional aid, subordination of loans to adherence to human rights and workers' rights. Bertrand Badie perfectly summarised this binding use of human rights by speaking of international diplomacy of human rights wavering between 'ethics and the will to power'.[28] The post-Cold War consensus on human rights has since then gradually broken apart, and the accusation of cultural imperialism has become a major criticism raised by the countries of the South. Some have denounced a new Western neocolonialism or imperialism, a vehicle for new 'civilising missions' conducted in the name of human rights and reflecting a typically Western cultural ethnocentrism: raising one's own values to the status of universal values and claiming that what is good for the West is good for the rest of the world. It is only when the populations in question, like the Arabic populations of Egypt and Tunisia, seize human rights for themselves that a non-hegemonic use of those rights seems to be at work and they discover their tremendous emancipatory potential.

That said, if one seeks to identify more closely one of the significant moments of the emergence of human rights issues and cultures after the Cold War, one might mention the first major international conference on human rights held in Vienna in 1993, which has already been discussed, as the event that incontrovertibly prompted the first big questions on this subject while it also gave rise to a major celebration of unity in this domain. The final declaration emphasises the renewed

[28] B. Badie, *La diplomatie des droits de l'homme. Entre éthique et volonté de puissance*, Paris: Fayard, 2002.

unity of the international community over human rights but also their indivisibility – which was in doubt after the adoption of the two separate Covenants in 1966. But at the Conference there was fierce opposition among state representatives over the cultural questions, and numerous demands were already foreshadowed pressing international human rights law to take better account of the cultures and values of each state. Some of the regional conferences in preparation for the Vienna Conference had already reflected this new spirit, particularly the Bangkok Conference of Asian countries and the Tunis Conference of African states. They led to final declarations fully reasserting the principle of universality of rights but also asking that national and regional cultural particularisms be better integrated in the definition and application of the rights. Point 5 of the Tunis Declaration recalled that 'no ready-made model can be prescribed at the universal level since the historical and cultural realities of each nation and the traditions, standards and values of each people cannot be disregarded'.[29]

Beyond certain political and legal offensives against human rights which are used by authoritarian or fundamentalist governments, there emerges a true and forceful concern for the necessary cultural adaptation of rights. The correlative demand by many non-Western states for recognition of and greater respect for their cultures, materialised in the 2005 UNESCO Convention on the diversity of cultural expression, could not but have repercussions on the way human rights are

---

[29] Final declaration of the regional meeting for Africa of the World Conference on Human Rights. A/Conf. 157/PC/57.

conceived and enforced. Besides, it has always been known, without actually taking it into account, that Asian and African societies and the many indigenous South American communities often reflect a community ideal that does not correspond to Western individualistic values enshrined in the instruments on human rights.

They have other ways of organising their solidarity, considering their relationships with religion, assuming responsibilities and expressing their dignity; so much so that they link the observance of individual rights with respect for legal obligations towards their families, their neighbourhoods, their communities, their religions or the state. These are not alienating features for the individual but, on the contrary, the blossoming in lived experience of these cultural, religious or community ties. Now, in the context of post-Cold War globalisation and the increased fear of seeing cultures under threat, such an essential dimension could no longer be ignored or disregarded, and accordingly its integration into the definition, interpretation and/or the application of human rights is called for

The highlighting of these new requirements then subjects international human rights law to a legal logic that shifts almost imperceptibly from a process of recognition of persons based on the assertion of an equal status and dignity of each human being, regardless of the cultural differences between individuals (1948 Declaration and 1966 Conventions), to a new stage of rights recognition based on cultural differences. The rights recognised in 1948 and 1966 were supposed to be universal; they represented an identical set of rights for all, which prohibited discrimination according to the culture and traditions of each people. Today, conversely, it is a matter of interpreting and adapting human rights so that they are compatible with the cultural particularisms of each people and take account of these positively without their being called into question. In other words, it is a matter of reaching a new stage at which we supposedly shift from formal equality to differentiated equality, in which people wish to be 'equal and different'.[30] Contemporary international law contains in this sense a promise of emancipation and recognition of each human being in what is simultaneously their equal dignity and their cultural difference.

The development of international human rights law within international law has been one of the major political, ideological and legal events of the last thirty years. Classical international law was an inter-state law that was both stigmatising and discriminatory, based on the hierarchy between cultures and civilisations, justifying complete inequality of status between states, peoples and individuals in the service of the European colonising/civilising venture. Contemporary international law, based ultimately on human rights, may well reflect not a simple cultural and legal shift but a real reversal, with recognition not just of the equal status and rights of individuals, peoples and states but also recognition of the equal dignity of their cultures and civilisations. The whole question remains, though, as to how to strike a balance between international human rights law and respect for cultures. Will

---

[30] See A. Touraine, *Pourrons-nous vivre ensemble? Egaux et différents*, Paris: Fayard, 1997.

international human rights law be supported on firmer mul-
ticultural bases than before, or is there a risk, on the pretext
of preserving everyone's cultural practices, of reintroducing
underlying tensions and eroding the feature that makes up the
essential part of human dignity?

CONCLUSION

We are witnessing a reconfiguration of international law within the international society that arose out of the Second World War and has become a post-colonial and post-Cold War world. This reconfiguration might seem disconcerting because it combines certain fundamental features of classical international law with new forms of amenability to law and new areas of intervention and regulation. Contemporary international law is the manifestation of an impetus that pervades international law which comes from its distant modern European origins and from the transformation of Western democracies after the Second World War. It is the accomplishment once again of a certain Western ethnocentrism, but which this time has confronted decolonisation, acculturation, cultural impregnation and globalisation. With this momentum, it now reflects a phenomenon of growing 'pan-legalism' because new rules of international law are constantly being produced without the old ones being abolished. It is now ubiquitous, intervening everywhere to govern the lives of states, peoples and individuals. It is still a liberal law of regulation while also being a welfarist, interventionist and multifunctional system of law. It is considered to be the guarantor of international peace, in the forms newly instituted by the UN Charter, while also being the guarantor of the freedoms of human beings, of their social rights, of the development of states, the preservation of the biosphere and the collective well-being of the world's population.

In an age characterised by the political reappraisal of law, the exponential, multifarious, disordered and fragmented development of international law reflects the growing complexity of international society and the national societies that it governs, and therefore a complexity of itself via a feedback effect. Care is required in interpreting these changes and recompositions of law because we have probably not yet taken their full measure nor questioned all of the postulates, consequences or alternatives. Moreover, the focus on this new configuration of contemporary international law produces as many problems as it does new models. It is a mixture of efficacy and powerlessness. Such an observation does not in itself discredit international law but it does demonstrate that, while the changes observed in this book are particularly interesting, they are problematic and invite us to maintain a constantly critical perspective on developments.

Textbooks

There are vast numbers of textbooks in most languages. For a complete review, see D. Carreau and F. Marrella, *Droit International*, 11th edn, Paris: Pedone, 2012, p. 27–30. Below are some of the main textbooks in French:

Alland, D. (ed.), *Droit International Public*, Paris: Puf, 2000.

Carreau, D. and Marrella, F., *Droit International*, 11th edn, Paris: Pedone, 2012.

Combacau, J. and Sur, S., *Droit International Public*, 9th edn, Paris: Montchrestien, 2010.

Decaux, E., *Droit International Public*, 6th edn, Paris: Dalloz, 2008.

Dupuy, P.-M. and Kerbrat, Y., *Droit International Public*, 10th edn, Paris: Dalloz, 2010.

Nguyen, Q. D., Daillier, P., Forteau, M. and Pellet, A., *Droit International Public*, 8th edn, Paris: LGDJ, 2009.

Rivier, R., *Droit International Public*, Paris: Puf, 2012.

Verhoeven, J., *Droit International Public*, Brussels: Larcier, 2000.

In English by the author:

Tourme Jouannet, Emmanuelle, *The Liberal-Welfarist Law of Nations. A History of International Law*, Cambridge University Press, 2012.

What is a Fair International Society? International Law between Development and Recognition? Oxford: Hart Publishing, 2013.

Collected courses, dictionaries and encylopedias

Recueil des Cours. Collected Courses of the Hague Academy of International Law Series. See especially the 'General Courses' given annually. www.ppl.nl/recueil.

Careau, D., P. Lagarde and H. Sybntet (eds.), *Encyclopédie Dalloz. Répertoire de Droit International*, Paris: Dalloz, 2004.

Kahn, Ph. and L. Vogel (eds.), *Jurisclasseur de Droit International*, www.lexisnexis.fr.

Salmon, J. (ed.), *Dictionnaire de Droit International Public*, Brussels: Bruylant, 2001.

Wolfrum, R. (ed.), *Max Planck Encyclopedia of Public International Law*, http://opil.ouplaw.com/home/EPIL.

INDEX